The world's
motor museums

Richard L. Knudson

by the same author
Adventurer's Road
The Trailblazers
Five Roads to Danger
Automobile Treasures
European Cars 1886–1914
The Motor Book
The Second Motor Book
A Toy for the Lion
The Vintage Car 1919–1930
Car Badges of the World
Sports Cars 1928–1940
Passenger Cars 1863–1904
Sports Cars 1907–1927
Passenger Cars 1905–1912
The Wild Roads
Sprint: Hillclimbs and Speed Trials
in Britain 1899–1925

T R Nicholson

The world's motor museums

with 130 black and white illustrations and 8 colour illustrations

J B Lippincott Company
Philadelphia and New York

Printed in Great Britain
Library of Congress Catalog Card
Number: 75–133454

Acknowledgements

The author and publisher offer their grateful thanks to all those in charge of the collections described for their kind co-operation in providing the data and illustrations in this book. They wish particularly to express their gratitude to the following for giving information and other assistance so generously: Mr W. Eric Allsop, Mr James Allward; Dr Giancarlo Amari, Mr Eric Bellamy and Mrs Erica Woodley of the Montagu Motor Museum, Mr Oluf Berrum, Mr Charles L. Betts Jr, Mr Chassaing de Borredon, Mr Richard Brigham, Mr George H. Brooks, Mrs N. K. Carr, Mr G. N. Georgano, Mr Antony Hannoyer, Mr Egon Hanus, Mr Eric Langton, Dr A. S. Lewerenz, Mr Marshall Naul, Mr Hans-Otto Neubauer, Mr J. S. P. Palmer, Mr Jackie Pichon, Mr Michael Pitts, Mr Jose Rodriguez-Vina, Mr Michael Sedgwick, Mr Hugh Taylor, Ing. W. Stiebling and Mr Michael Worthington-Willams.

Contents

Foreword

Motor museums have now become an integral part, not only of the worldwide Veteran and Vintage movement, but also of the whole history of civilization.

Twenty years ago such institutions were the exception rather than the rule. A few far-sighted manufacturers, notably Daimler-Benz of Untertürkheim, were already putting by vital exhibits for posterity, but otherwise the preservation of road transport relics was left to the national technical museums of the world. These were inevitably handicapped by their wide terms of reference, for if one has to embrace the entire corpus of technology, only a small corner can be dedicated to the motorcar, a line of development which had barely been born when the machine age first became worthy of commemoration. These early museums also suffered from a self-consciously educational aura: one 'did' them as a schoolboy, and one wrote essays about them afterwards. In such an atmosphere it was hard to associate a gently mouldering Benz 'Velo' or early wheel-steered Panhard either with the pioneering days it symbolized, or as the ancestor of the Austins, Citroëns, Opels, Fiats, and Chevrolets in the street outside.

Such cultural mausolea still exist, but with the meteoric rise of interest in early and historic vehicles has come a recognition of the part played in history by mechanized road transport. Clubs and museums are complementary, and the museum mentality is fading away. No longer do the doors clang shut behind an exhibit, with the consequence that it never runs again under its own power. While such a fate is undoubtedly the right one for a handful of the most fragile and specialized machinery, cars were made to be used, and it has always been my policy to run my own collection in rallies. There is no better way of ensuring a crowd, even on the museum floor, than by starting a car up and driving it out on to the road.

The 'living museum' philosophy has had other and more important effects. Obviously cars preserved for posterity cannot be lent out indiscriminately to enthusiasts, but the museums can play their part by offering research and library services. They can also introduce a cohesive theme into the pattern of their exhibits. In the early days of the motor-museum cult one could not help wondering if at least some of the vehicles on display were present simply 'because they were there'. Even now opinions differ as to what a museum should contain, and at the risk of introducing a personal viewpoint I would say that its primary function should be to tell the story of mechanized road transport in its most representative form. Such a credo will involve a certain degree of self-discipline: one has to eschew the glamour attendant upon specializing in racing cars, or the charm of certain periods– the brass-bound barbarities of the pre-1905 era, the glorious baroque of the so-called Edwardians, and the sheer sartorial magnificence of the early 1930s classics. Fords, Chevrolets, Morris Cowleys, and the like are equally significant, and many more people cut their motoring teeth on them.

None the less, there is scope for the specialist in the world of the museum, just as there is elsewhere in the movement, and within the pages of Mr. Nicholson's book will be found details of institutions large and small, devoted to fire-fighting equipment, to motor cycles, to exhibits of largely national character, to individual *marques*, and even (in the case of West Berlin's Vergaser Museum) to the history of the carburettor. That this work is needed is shown by the attendances they attract–a steady half a million a year at Beaulieu is matched by some most impressive figures from abroad, for instance one-and-a-half million a year at the Henry Ford Collection in Dearborn, not to mention ever-growing support for the magnificent Harrah museum at Reno, which boasted over 1,300 cars last time I was there.

Some readers may prefer their cars in action to the static, but this guide has performed an admirable service: while one hesitates to be too dogmatic, it would surprise me if an enthusiast with a rare series-production model will not find

that one of the museums listed by Mr. Nicholson does not possess a similar example, and thus tourists will be able to pick up some information of immediately practical value as well as feasting their eyes on relics of infinite variety, technical interest, and pure nostalgic appeal.

Montagu of Beaulieu

Introduction

The multiplication over the past ten years or so of museums devoted to, or including a significant collection of, motor vehicles has been remarkable, particularly in Europe, where there were perhaps 20 in 1959, 40 in 1962, and over 80 now. The increase has not been in the numbers of collections belonging to national, state or regional museums of an official character, which have existed in industrialized nations ever since the motor vehicle had developed enough to justify its earliest manifestations going into museums; i.e. since soon after the turn of the century. Individual company's museums have existed for nearly as long, though they were not, and are not, invariably open to the public. The spread has come with the world-wide popularity of old vehicles as public entertainment. Since the Second World War, and especially in the last 15 or 20 years, cars and motor cycles (and more recently commercial and public service vehicles) have become things to be searched for, restored, run on the road, and generally treasured by private individuals as a hobby. *En masse*, they have become public spectacles, their gatherings watched by television cameras, film units, the newspapers, and spectators in their tens or hundreds of thousands, who could never hope to own one of these increasingly rare and expensive luxuries, but who can enjoy them vicariously, at meetings—or in museums. The great majority of today's motor museums are private collections recently opened to the public, run usually on a commercial basis, occasionally as a private educational service, or with a mixture of motives. They comprise a nucleus that was the owner's original collection, augmented by purchases or loans since the public museum was launched. In the United States and Canada in particular, where there are probably around 100 of them in all, the automotive collection will often be only a part of a folk or local industries and crafts museum, included because of the relevance or the popular 'pull' of early vehicles.

Over 170 open museums in 26 countries from Ireland to Japan and from the Soviet Union to New Zealand, are noted in this book, but even so, it cannot safely be claimed that all in existence are mentioned. There are several reasons for this. Partly it is a question of definition. The collections described here are those that are open to the public as a matter of course at certain seasons and between fixed hours–not just by appointment or as a special favour on request. A great many that set out to attract visitors to tourist resorts are open in the local holiday season only: these are included. By 'motor vehicles' is meant passenger and competition cars, motor cycles, and commercial and public service vehicles. Armoured fighting vehicles, agricultural vehicles and tramcars, though technically road-going, are not included, because tracked machines or those running on rails are too remote from the motor vehicle proper. At the same time, some of the museums here will include some of these types; also, specialized museums devoted to important components of the motor vehicle such as engines and carburettors are included. Descriptions of cars are given more prominence than descriptions of motor cycles or other vehicles. This is because in the museum world, the former are by far the more popular and numerous. Unless its vehicles are of special importance, a museum with only one or two on show is not included. Generally speaking, its vehicle collection must be more than purely incidental to the rest of its exhibits in order for it to qualify as a 'motor museum'.

The other limiting factor has been the impossibility of obtaining data even on all the collections within the above definitions. While the author has done his best to compile a complete roster of collections before starting to write the book, his contacts, though worldwide, were not people who had made a special study of museums, and there are no existing published lists that are both up to date and complete. In any case, new ones are opening literally every day. Many of the museums written to did not reply, in spite of repeated enquiries. This could be because of lack of interest on their part, or because they no longer existed. The commercially-run museum is

exceedingly ephemeral. Their lives tend to be short, especially in the United States. It can seldom be safely assumed that such a museum open two years ago is still open today.

This has led to the division of the museums in this book into categories. Those entries marked with one star are known to have been in existence at the time of writing, but did not reply to enquiries. Those with two stars are collections whose existence later than 1968 could not be proved; those with three stars, 1967; and those with four, 1966. If the latest evidence for the existence of a commercial collection open to the public dates back to 1965 or earlier, it has been excluded, because the risk of its being closed is too high for its inclusion to have any point. This system is designed as a general guide only; intending visitors are strongly advised to make sure if a museum is open before making what may be a fruitless journey. There are other good reasons for making preliminary contact. Opening times and seasons (even where they were supplied in full) often change. Many exhibits are on loan only and may have been reclaimed by their owners; they could be out on hire, or attending a meeting, or be in store, or in the workshop, or sold. Finally, the dates attributed to vehicles may be changed. (Those given in this book were as supplied by the collections concerned.)

It was impossible, in the compass of a book of reasonable length and price, to list all the exhibits of every museum mentioned, which can run into four figures. In any case, most museums did not supply the author with full lists, one reason being that their exhibits are constantly changing. For the same reasons, it was only possible to provide a representative selection of illustrations.

The author hopes that these limitations will be tolerated by the users of this book, which is intended to provide a general picture of today's motor museums, and a guide to the majority of them.

Restoring an old car

It is the policy of most collections, especially those which are run partly or wholly on a commercial basis, to restore their acquisitions as nearly as possible to the condition in which they left their factories. Some museums put exhibits on display before restoration, and a few don't bother at all, perhaps on grounds of lack of money or knowledge or skill, sometimes claiming by way of excuse that, beyond repairing actual breakages and removing anachronisms, restoration is unjustifiable – the car ceases to be original. Much more than mechanical skill is needed for an accurate restoration: long research and dedicated scholarship are often called for, and not every museum has access to, or understands the need for, this sort of expertise, which needs libraries as well as researchers.

There is a genuine and deep division of opinion among restorers as to what qualifies as correct restoration, and what is 'originality'. If upholstery is shabby and moth-eaten, should it simply be refurbished and repaired, and left substantially in the state in which it arrived, or should it be completely renewed with the correct materials and upholstering techniques? Should the car's crankshaft big end bearings be remetalled in the original material, which was, perhaps, known to last only a short distance when the car was new, owing to a fault of design, or should a better, perhaps modern, material be used so that the car may be driven at exhibitions and meetings? (Here another, but unrelated, question of policy arises – whether or not to run the cars. Will they not last longer as static museum exhibits?) Sometimes where expendables are involved – as in the case of tires and sparking plugs, for instance – there is no question of absolute originality, since parts to the exact original specifications and material are unobtainable: but there is plenty of other room for differences of opinion.

Here are three accounts of how different museums in different countries work, very kindly provided for this book by the museums concerned. The differences revealed are of emphasis rather than of principle.

The Daimler-Benz Museum, Stuttgart-Untertürkheim

Before beginning restoration work on veteran cars, particularly those made before the turn of the century, it is advisable to take photographs, both general and close-up, so that later, when the parts are being replaced, it will be possible to compare their condition before and after renovation, as well as their position on the car.

To enable the costs of such restoration work to be determined later, the total time spent, materials used, new parts, work done by outside firms, etc., must be accurately assessed.

The restoration begins by dividing the vehicle into its main component parts: engine – transmission – chassis – bodywork. If, when one runs the engine, it seems to have sufficient compression, and the moving parts (especially the big end bearings and the main bearings) are in order, it will be sufficient if the engine is cleaned inside and out. When the overhaul of the engine is completed, it should be painted, taking care that all the paints used, including all ornaments if any, correspond to the original. If serious defects are found in the engine, it would be advisable to entrust a firm of repair specialists with its reconditioning. In most cases grinding of the crank pins is necessary, followed by the making of new main and big end bearings.

If the transmission is also to be overhauled, it is recommended that one takes photographs or makes sketches which show the steps necessary for rebuilding. This recommendation applies to the dismantling of all units, no matter how simple their rebuilding may appear at the outset. Transmission gear wheels, which have to be renovated or replaced, must as far as possible be made from the same material and have the same surface treatment as the originals.

All iron parts which are removed from the body, including the radiator and fuel and lubricant tanks, must be cleaned on the outside, and (even more important) on the inside. If it is found that the inside of any of these containers is thickly coated, that this cannot be removed by flushing, and that there is the possibility of this coating later causing trouble, one is advised to proceed in the following manner: Cut a large hole in the top of the tank so as to allow it to be cleaned. The part that has been cut out can be later welded back into place. When carrying out this work one should take great care; it is advisable to fill the tank as far as possible with water, so that only the part to be welded remains clear of the water. When carrying out the cleaning by mechanical means, one should wear some sort of respirator.

If the containers are so badly rusted that it is questionable whether they are serviceable, it is better to replace them by new containers made from the same material. Where deep rusting has occurred, the rust must be removed by grinding, and round parts must be turned on a lathe. Damaged parts which no longer possess the necessary strength should be reconditioned as new. When doing this work, pins and bolts, which are subject to greater stresses, should correspond to the original part in workmanship, strength and in the treatment they have received. Shafts which are below the tolerance limit can be made serviceable by hard-chroming and regrinding. All plain metal parts except for bearing surfaces should always be treated with rust protection coating. When the engine, transmission, axles, wheels, fuel and coolant tanks are removed, only the bare bodywork is left.

If entire sections of the frame have to be replaced because the wood is rotten or the iron platework has rusted through, or because parts are no longer serviceable, these must be carefully dismantled so that they can be used as templates for the new parts.

If the paintwork needs to be renewed, the old paint should be removed either by scraping or using paint remover. When doing this it is important to ascertain what the original colour was, and in addition, the pattern of the lining and decorative effects. The vehicle must certainly be restored to its pristine colours; in most cases it will be found that several coats of paint have been used. When the old paint has been removed, the parts have to be ground down, primed and if

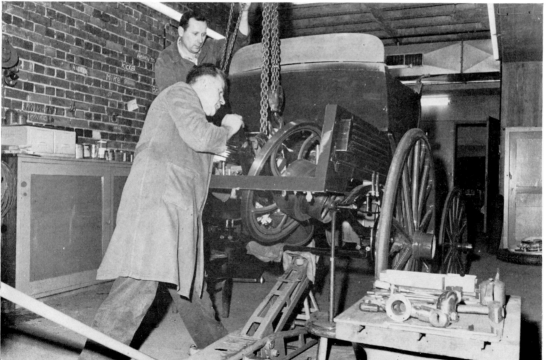

A Benz is reconstructed. Courtesy Daimler-Benz Museum, Stuttgart

necessary smoothed, filled and then sanded down again.

For wooden parts, a synthetic resin or oil-based paint is used, as these types give the best protection.

In many cases, parts of the car such as tanks, radiator, fuel and oil lines which are made out of copper or brass become tarnished in the course of time. These parts should be cleaned, polished and then treated with colourless varnish to prevent discoloration.

Many cars have decorative lining on their wheel spokes, springs and even on the engine; it should be reproduced in the same manner and colour as on the original vehicle.

When re-nickelling parts, only those parts should be treated that were so finished originally.

It happens sometimes that old cars no longer have the same size of wheels as those originally fitted, as original tires can no longer be obtained. In such cases it is imperative that the wheels be replaced by those of the original size. The hubs can usually be re-used. Where the wooden spokes have to be replaced in order to bring the wheel to its original diameter, dry well-seasoned acacia, ash or, if they are unobtainable, beech are used. The making of wooden spokes is best done by a coach-maker of the old school.

In some cases one will also have to have new wheel rims made, where the original type is no longer available. In most cases this is no easy task, as the tools, jigs and fixtures for such rims are no longer in existence and will have to be improvised. Specialised firms can undertake the making of the rims from sketches.

Rims should only be made when the tires are to hand or when a sample rim can be placed at the disposal of the tire firm. Only when the rim has been procured is it possible for the wooden spoked wheel to be made.

It can be difficult when the lamps are missing. If one has them made, or acquires them, one must consider to which period the car belongs, and whether candle, carbide or electric lights were used. Carbide lighting needed special acetylene generators, which are not so easy to obtain. Lamps and lights have in most cases to be copied, and this applies also to the glass in four-cornered lamps, which had a 10 mm. bevel around the edges. Hooters and horns, when they

can be obtained, are often badly dented, but it is amazing how such items can be restored to good condition in the hands of craftsmen.

As the upholstery is in clear view, it contributes greatly to giving period character to the vehicle. If the leatherwork of the car is still good and undamaged, it is usually sufficient to renovate it by using a suitable leather paint. If, on the other hand, the upholstery has to be completely renewed, the old pieces of upholstery should be saved as a sample and the vehicle re-covered in the same way, and if possible, with the same leather and colour as on the original. When doing this, the upholstery should look as though it has been used.

The materials used for tops are often so antiquated and brittle that they have to be renewed. In the same way, the type of material and colour used on the original vehicle should be chosen.

Efforts should be made especially to restore objects which appear of secondary importance to their original condition; it pays to do so.

Renovation is not complete until the car is roadworthy again. After the engine has completed a proving test, a trial run is undertaken so as to check the fuel and cooling systems. The transmission has also to be tested; during this test the vehicle should be driven in all the gears. Most important is the checking of the brakes, so that when test drives are made there is no possibility of an accident.

Museo dell' Automobile Carlo Biscaretti di Ruffia, Turin

Restoration is one of the most complex problems facing collectors and lovers of period cars. It often happens that the old vehicles that one prepares to restore have been completely abandoned for a number of years, perhaps after hard and careless use in their later years, when they were already regarded as finished. In such a case delicate and precise work is required to put the car back into efficient working order and to restore it to its old splendour, bearing in mind the double objective: mechanics and aesthetics.

The results seen at meetings of veteran cars are sometimes deceptive, as one notices out-of-place additions and modifications, made through ignorance or out of a desire to put the car back into shape more quickly and easily. It may happen that engines originally fitted with hot-tube ignition are running with electric ignition, and one may find modern carburettors fitted to sixty-year-old cars.

One must take into account, however, the now-frequent use of period cars in gruelling competitions, with the consequent likelihood of rapid depreciation, above all of the older parts.

Whoever considers a restoration job should first of all face the question of tires. Leaving aside the high cost involved, the problem can be resolved by approaching tire manufacturers who have diligently recovered or reconstructed the original moulds. Tires are thus one of the few components that are allowed to be of recent manufacture, owing to the impossibility of preserving the originals.

On the subject of replacements, one cannot help at times replacing the clutch, and sometimes also the ball-bearings, if any. As far as connecting-rods, pistons, shafts and gears are concerned one must be more severe, although the reconstruction of these parts requires delicacy, and also research. A damaged yet well-repaired gearbox appreciates more than a new one.

Exceptional patience and ability are also required to restore to efficient order parts such as the water-pump, magneto, etc., which may be irreplaceable and always in poor condition after prolonged use. Brakes and clutches generally benefit from new linings, and here is another case where the use of modern products is tolerated.

Still more abuses are committed against the lighting system, in the name of practicality. Modern headlights obviously give more security than old ones, if they are electric, and they are certainly less complicated than the acetylene type. There remains, however, the problem of tracking down lamps of the period, so as to achieve restoration. Unfortunately most of these go to satisfy the appetites of the salvage hunters, as one can see in most car graveyards.

It becomes very difficult to equip an old car if the principal accessories are lacking. In certain cases industries are created for the manufacture of parts identical in all respects to the originals. To cite an example, horns of complex and intricate type are manufactured in India and sold in England. Electrical components are not so easy to reproduce. Nevertheless one can find skilful craftsmen capable of remaking instruments and brass lamps as new, even if the originals are badly damaged.

The reconstruction of bodywork gives rise to a variety of difficulties, the first of which is discovering the body's original form, taking into account successive modifications that may have taken place. It is also a question of tracking down the correct materials and using, as far as possible, the working techniques of the period.

Special woods and the cabinet-makers capable of working them are still to be found (even if the work is hard). The fashion for wood, as a decorative as well as a structural element in car bodies, reached its peak in the years preceding the First World War, when cars became accepted as a comfortable means of transport. This was the time of maximum splendour in interiors: velvets, silks, lace and 'petit point' were often used. Unfortunately they are difficult to replace today, and only a few are repairable, and then need extreme care. Fortunately there are special chemical products to reduce damage caused by weather and negligence: humidity, dust and stains of all types. The task of putting a beautiful interior in order can involve tremendous fatigue, but it is rewarded with great satisfaction.

There are no insurmountable problems connected with exteriors; although some can turn out to be difficult. Today, for example, there are few (if any) craftsmen capable of producing a leather wing. But sometimes parts of the bodywork are in aluminium – for example wings and hoods – and in such cases the difficulties are reduced. Brass is unusual today, yet it can be worked well and easily. It is necessary to remember to avoid substituting one metal for another, to avoid spoiling the authenticity of the vehicle.

The greatest difficulty remains that of finding information, and here museums play an important role. One should go to them either in search of documentation, or to see, if one is lucky, a similar vehicle in the collection. One should avoid at all costs repainting by spray-gun a car which was originally painted by brush. One should (above all) try to restore the elegant striping in contrasting colours which frequently ornaments old cars.

It is undoubtedly permissible to use all the 'beauty products' put on the market today for modern cars, for the purpose of preserving the old ones; for example some waxes for the paintwork, and others for polishing metal. A lot can be said for the silicon-based compounds used to protect hides, and those intended for woodwork. A spray-on waterproofing treatment for interior trim exists: it is invisible and should give protection not only against stains and dust, but also against moths and mould.

Harrah's Automobile Collection, Reno, Nevada

Once a car has been acquired and earmarked for restoration, it is completely disassembled in the main shop and its many parts directed to the various shops. Seats and interior fabrics go to the upholsterers, plated surfaces to the metal shop and repairers, body to the body shop, and so on. After the parts are steam-cleaned and sandblasted, they are restored step by step according to factory specifications dictated by the Collection's research department. Then, when they have been repaired, the components are funnelled back to the main restoration shop for final assembly.

After an automobile is acquired, the research department moves to establish the history of the car. This involves more sleuthing for information pertinent to the restoration. In an effort to locate specific missing or unrestorable parts, advertising is placed in special publications which reach thousands of old-car enthusiasts.

Since many restorations are in progress here simultaneously, the time involved in locating spare parts is not critical. Should any one job be held up for whatever reason, the collective effort is

The body shop. Courtesy Harrah's Automobile Collection, Reno, Nevada

simply turned to other projects. In this way the programme is geared to move ahead on a schedule from day to day.

At Harrah's Automobile Collection the objective is to return the car to its original factory specifications; not only its exterior appearance but the engine and moving parts as well. The restored car must run as well and look exactly as it did the day it rolled off the factory floor.

Since authenticity is the key to all restoration activity, research experts function as the nerve centre. In addition to conducting preliminary inspection reports, the researchers prepare restoration manuals for other departments involved in the restoration, follow up with daily inspection of work, and daily index incoming literature.

While it may have been difficult enough to find a specific model of car, it is even harder to locate corresponding literature, manuals and photographs of the cars which are used as guides during the restoration process. The hub of the research department is the library. Much of the information to be found here – in thousands of automotive books, magazines, sales catalogues, operation manuals, and photographs – is catalogued and indexed in card files for rapid reference.

The end result of this precise team effort at Harrah's is a complete car — but the car must still prove itself before the job is accepted. Performance is checked against factory specifications and no car is approved without first undergoing a road test. Before a car is subjected to the final test it must be driven a minimum number of miles to establish its reliability. If the car being tested fails to perform as specified, it is returned to the shop, where its shortcomings are determined and corrected. If it passes all requirements for authenticity, performance and appearance, the automobile is recorded as a 'Gold Star' restoration, the highest recognition that can be achieved – and the car takes a spot in automotive history, as preserved by Harrah's Automobile Collection.

Museums due to be opened

These collections should be approached with extreme caution, since they were not open to the public at the time of writing. They are included because plans have been made to open them before or around the publication date of this book. All available details are given.

SPAIN
Musée Francais de la Carrosserie,
Port Andraitx,
Mallorca

Francisco de la Rocha Hispano-Suiza collection,
Madrid

HOLLAND
Lips Automobile Museum,
Drunen
Over 100 cars, including 1902 four-wheel-drive Spyker.

Batavus Bicycle and Automobile Museum,
Heerenveen, near Sneek,
Friesland

BELGIUM
Automobielmuzeum van Belgie te
Houthalen-Limburg
An extension of the Ghislain Mahy Collection
Ghent (q.v.)

ARGENTINA

Museo Automovil Club Argentino,
Lujan
Open summer 12.30–17.30 winter 12.00–17.00
Argentina has a remarkable number of cars
surviving from the pioneer days of the automobile,
and about two dozen of the most notable of these,
albeit unrestored, are to be found in the
Automobile Club of Argentina's collection at
Lujan. There are two Daimlers, at least one of
them from the 1880s or early 1890s; Holsman,
International Harvester, and Schacht buggies
from America; a 1908 Fiat, two Cadillacs of 1904
and 1912; 1904 and 1908 Panhard-Levassors; and
a 1911 Wanderer. There is also an Iruam of 1927,
built in Argentina.

Museo Historico del Norte,
Salta
Opening seasons and times not communicated
This museum, run by the Argentine Ministry of
Education, possesses a Renault of 1910.

* * *

Museo Historico Regional de la Colonia
San José, Urquiza 378,
San José, Dept. Colon,
Entre Rios
*Open every day except Monday 8.00–12.00,
14.00–18.00*
The half-dozen or so cars in this museum are all
earlier than 1912; there are also horsedrawn
vehicles from 1857, and exhibits illustrating
regional and colonial history.

Daimler, ca. 1887. Wrongly labelled a Benz. Courtesy Museo Automovil Club Argentino, Lujan, Argentina

Renault, 1911. Courtesy Museo Automovil Club Argentino, Lujan, Argentina

AUSTRALIA
New South Wales

Bronk's Motor Museum,
17 Military Road,
Watson's Bay,
Sydney,
New South Wales
Open every day except Tuesday 11.00–18.00
There are about 20 cars on show here, including 1906 Holsman, 1911 Bedelia, 1920 Darracq, 1923 Hotchkiss, and 1930 Packard. There are also half a dozen motor cycles, such as a 1906 FN, 1919 Neracar, 1922 Ace, and 1925 Moto Guzzi.

Queensland

Gilltraps Auto Museum,
Kirra,
Gold Coast,
Queensland
Open every day except Christmas Day and Good Friday 8.00–17.00
The late George Gilltrap's collection of cars, commercial vehicles, fire engines, motor cycles, bicycles, locomotives, horsedrawn carriages and aircraft is the most notable transportation museum in Australia that is open to the public. It was started in New Zealand, but moved to Queensland in 1959. The pre-Second World War cars it contains

Model T Ford, 1912. Courtesy Bronk's Motor Museum, Sydney, New South Wales, Australia

number about 70, plus around a dozen motor cycles. The best-known among the former is no doubt the 1904 Darracq that took part in the film *Genevieve*, but exceeding it in historical and technical interest are the 1902 Albion, 1905 Russell from Canada, 1908 Vulcan, 1911 Napier, 1913 Unic charabanc, 1914 Twombley, and 1918 Australian Six – a representative of the most successful Australian make prior to the coming of the Holden. From the 1920s are a 1922 Benz, 1923 Lanchester, 1925 Isotta-Fraschini, and a 1926 Stearns-Knight. The more modern items of interest include one of the first Holdens of 1948, and a 1955 Ferrari Grand Prix car.

South Australia

Birdwood Mill Museum,
Birdwood,
South Australia
Opening seasons and times not communicated
Most of the cars in this collection are of American origin, reflecting the fact that the American car was the favoured import of most Australians in the early days. Among some 12 machines, the most interesting are a 1914 Dixi, a 1926 Packard, the chassis of a 19th-century Peugeot, and a La Salle that is said to have been one of General MacArthur's wartime staff cars. There are over 60 motor cycles, including a 1902 Minerva.

Panhard-Levassor, 1903. Courtesy Gilltraps Auto Museum, Kirra, Queensland, Australia

Victoria

Antique Car and Folk Museum,
Princes Highway,
Lakes Entrance 3909,
Victoria
Open every day 10.00–22.00

Mr Raymond Standerwick's museum shows horsedrawn vehicles, agricultural machinery, traction engines, tractors, and motor cycles as well as motor cars, of which there are upwards of 30. Most of these are American. They include an IHC Buggy of 1909, 1917 Dodge, 1918 and 1928 Buick, 1923 Ford, 1926 Studebaker, 1927 Dodge and Diana, 1928 Falcon Knight (a rarity, this), 1933 Nash and 1928 Graham Paige. There are four seldom-seen European cars in the shape of a 1912 Opel, 1921 Minerva, 1924 Panhard-Levassor and 1930 Horch; but the commercial vehicles run them close in interest–1911 Pierce-Arrow and 1912 Garford fire engines, 1912 Hercules truck, 1913 Model T Ford baker's van, and 1920 Yellow Cab. The motor cycles take in 1901 Precision and Minerva, two more Minervas of 1905 and 1909, 1913 Triumph, 1917 Indian, 1922 New Imperial, and 1926 Harley-Davidson.

Institute of Applied Science of Victoria,
304–328 Swanston Street,
Melbourne,
Victoria
Opening seasons and times not communicated

The Institute has few motor vehicles, but these, most of them, are of outstanding interest. The most notable is certainly the 1896 Thomson steamer, the first car to be built in Australia. Then there is the Chicago-built Hertel of 1899; one of the first imported cars. From the 1920s, the collection has (though not yet on show) a Fiat 501 of 1926 and a real rarity in the shape of a 1923 Gräf und Stift from Austria.

*

Holden Agency,
Colac,
Victoria
Opening seasons and times not communicated

This collection, owned by Mr Parker, is known to exist, but no details were forthcoming at the time of writing.

Opel, 1912. Courtesy Antique Car and Folk Museum, Lakes Entrance, Victoria, Australia

IHC 1909. Courtesy Antique Car and Folk Museum, Lakes Entrance, Victoria, Australia

Panhard-Levassor, 1924. Courtesy Antique Car and Folk Museum, Lakes Entrance, Victoria, Australia

Thomson steamer, 1896. Courtesy Institute of Applied Science of Victoria, Australia

1886 Benz (foreground), 1886 Daimler (background). Courtesy Daimler-Benz Museum, Stuttgart, German Federal Republic

Clément-Panhard, 1900. Courtesy Cheddar Motor Museum, Cheddar, England

Fondu, 1906. Courtesy Ghislain Mahy Collection, Ghent, Belgium

Itala, 1907, that won the Peking-Paris Trial. Courtesy Museo dell'Automobile Carlo Biscaretti di Ruffia, Turin, Italy

Maserati, 1950. Courtesy Museu do Automovel, Caramulo, Portugal

1918 Buick. Courtesy Car and Folk Museum, Lakes Entrance, Victoria, Australia

Cars outside the Chateau de Rochetaillée: Left to right: 1908 Sizaire-Naudin, 1913 Clément-Bayard, 1912 Leon Bollée. Courtesy Musée Francais de l'Automobile, Rochetaillée-sur-Saône, France

Rumpler, ca. 1921. Courtesy Early American Museum, Silver Springs, Florida

Western Australia

P. W. Markham's Antique Auto Museum,
76 Flynn Street,
Wembley,
Western Australia
Open every day except Saturday 14.00–17.00
Founded in 1963, this collection, one of the finest
in the Southern Hemisphere, contains vehicles
ranging from an 1843 horsedrawn landau and a
number of motor cycles dating from 1904, to
around 40 cars. The latter embrace such rarities
as an 1898 Star, 1906 Germain and 1909 Minerva
from Belgium, a 1910 BSA, a Nazzaro of 1913, one
of the great Model 48 Locomobiles, this one of
1914, a 1921 Stanley steamer, and 1923 Itala.

Star, 1898. Courtesy Markham's Antique Auto Museum, Wembley, Western Australia

Rolls Royce, 1912. Courtesy Markham's Antique
Auto Museum, Wembley, Western Australia

Auburn, 1927. Courtesy Markham's Antique Auto
Museum, Wembley, Western Australia

Sizaire-Naudin, 1908. Courtesy Markham's Antique Auto Museum, Wembley, Western Australia

AUSTRIA

Technisches Museum für Industrie und Gewerbe,
Mariahilferstrasse 212,
1140 Vienna XIV
Open every day except Monday and weekends
October–April 9.00–13.00
May–September 14.00–16.00
The road transport section of the Vienna
Technical Museum contains bicycles, motor
cycles and cars from several countries, but
naturally the emphasis is on products either of
Austria or of the countries that were part of the
Austro-Hungarian empire. The most notable
machine shown is the Markus car attributed to
1875; said to be the world's oldest running internal-
combustion-engined vehicle. Here, too, are an
1886 Benz three-wheeler, other Benzes of 1887
and 1893, an 1894 Daimler, and a 1955 Grand Prix
Mercedes-Benz from Germany; a 1903 Piccolo, a
1900 Locomobile steamer from America, and a
French Serpollet steamer of 1897 and Voisin of
1925. Apart from the Markus, Austria is
represented by the Gräf of about 1898, the 1899
Nesselsdorf from Moravia, the 1900 Braun
voiturette, three electric and petrol-electric
vehicles on the Lohner-Porsche system, a
Knoller steamer, a 1911 Gräf und Stift, a Perl of
1925–6, a 1938 Steyr, and several commercial
vehicles and chassis.

Heeresgeschichtliches Museum,
The Arsenal,
Vienna 3
Open every day except Friday 10.00–16.00
There is only one motor car on show in this
museum, but it is of historic interest to the world
as a whole, if not to the motoring world. It is the
Gräf und Stift in which the Archduke Franz
Ferdinand and his wife were murdered at Sarajevo
in 1914; the event which precipitated, if it did not
cause, the Austrian attack on Serbia that began
the First World War. The car still displays its
bullet holes.

Gräf und Stift, 1912, in which the Archduke Franz Ferdinand and his wife were assassinated at Sarajevo, 1914. Courtesy Heeresgeschichtliches Museum, Vienna, Austria

Model N Ford, 1906. Courtesy Ghislain Mahy Collection, Ghent, Belgium

Rennmaschinen-Sammlung Brandstetter,
Brunngasse 23
St Polten
Open every day except Sundays 8.00–17.00
Walter Brandstetter's collection of over 30 motor
cycles concentrates on the machines ridden by
Austrian champions between 1922 and 1939.

BELGIUM

Ghislain Mahy Collection,
Watersportbaau,
Ghent
Opening seasons and times not communicated
The great Mahy collection that used to be housed
in the Garage Fiat in Ghent, and was not open to
any casual visitor, has now been broken up and
spread under more than one roof. At the time of
writing, the only public museum to show Mahy
cars is that named, where about 100 cars are
exhibited. It was planned that, in 1970, more Mahy
cars shall go to a new museum, the
Automobielmuzeum van Belgie te
Houthalen-Limburg.

BRAZIL

Museu Paulista de Antiguidades Mecanicas,
Caçapava,
Sao Paulo
Open every day 8.00–18.00
The only museum of transport open to the public
of Brazil at the time of writing is that owned by
Dr Roberto Eduardo Lee, whose collection of
cars numbers about 46. It concentrates upon the
'classics' of automotive history, and presents a
very distinguished display. On show are a Turcat-
Méry of about 1903 (a chassis only), an Alfonso
XIII Hispano-Suiza of around 1911, a Type RL
Alfa Romeo of 1924, a P3 Grand Prix car, and a
2300 six-cylinder chassis of *circa* 1936, two
Bugattis—the rare Type 38 and the even rarer
Type 52 electric Grand Prix miniature for
children—four Rolls-Royces, no fewer than seven
Packards, including a 12-cylinder of 1937, and a
Mercedes-Benz 500K. Other exhibits include three
horsedrawn carriages, and ten car engines.

Delahaye fire engine, 1907. Courtesy Ghislain Mahy Collection, Ghent, Belgium

CANADA
Alberta

Western Canadian Pioneer Museum
(Reynolds Museum),
Wetaskiwin,
Alberta
Open every day May–September 10.00–17.00
The Western Canadian Pioneer Museum shows
every side of pioneering life in Canada, from cars,
trucks and fire trucks to steam engines, aircraft,
horsedrawn vehicles, agricultural machinery,
household furniture and guns. The vehicles of all
kinds total about 700, of which 420 are motor
vehicles. Among the rarer and most interesting
cars are a 1909 IHC Autowagon, a 12-cylinder
National of 1917, 1912 Locomobile, front wheel
drive Cords of 1929 and 1936, 1911 Hupp-Yeats and
1908 Baker electrics, a Brooks steamer of 1924 and
a 1907 Tudhope-McIntyre from Canada, a Russell
(another Canadian make), the 1899 Florida-built
Innes, a six-cylinder Winton of 1915, a Wolverine,
a 1924 Sunbeam, and a 1908 Rochet-Schneider.

Manitoba

Elkhorn Manitoba Automobile Museum,
Provincial Trunk Highway 1,
Elkhorn,
Manitoba
Open every day May–October
This large collection of over 100 vehicles, of which
about 40 are on show, takes in two examples of
1912 EMF and Flanders, a 1908 Reo, 1909
Hupmobile, 1913 Case, 1914 Briscoe, one of the
very rare V8 Chevrolets of 1918–9, a McLaughlin
Buick of the same year and another Canadian car,
the 1913 Russell Knight. There are exhibits of
steam vehicles and farm machinery as well.

Ontario

Antique Auto Museum,
1871 Falls Avenue,
Niagara Falls,
Ontario
Open every day
This museum concentrates upon cars owned or
used by celebrities, but like other Canadian

Locomobile, 1912. Courtesy Western Canadian Pioneer Museum, Wetaskiwin, Alberta, Canada

collections, features cars of Canadian make as well. Among the former are a 1939 Horch said to have been used by Field-Marshal Rommel, a 1910 Rolls-Royce that belonged to the Duke of Windsor when Prince of Wales, Al Capone's 1928 Cadillac, Charles Lindbergh's Packard of 1927, the Lancia Astura of Benito Mussolini, and the late President Kennedy's 1963 Lincoln Continental. Canadian cars include the 'one-off' Victorian of 1896, 1916 Bartlett, 1915 Galt, 1920 McLaughlin, 1926 Brooks steamer, and two vehicles from the Tudhope Carriage Company: a 1906 Tudhope McIntyre Auto Buggy, and a 1909 Tudhope speedster. There are over 50 cars in all.

Canadian Automotive Museum,
99 Simcoe Street South,
Oshawa,
Ontario
Open every day Monday–Friday 10.00–17.00 Saturday 10.00–18.00 Sunday 12.00–18.00
Unlike most museums containing Canadian motor cars, that at Oshawa is devoted mostly to them

(appropriately enough, since the city has powerful associations with the automobile industry), and it is an educational rather than a profit-making concern, devoted to the history of the Canadian motor industry. All but a handful of the 30 vehicles shown either originated in or were assembled in Canada. The 1898 Redpath Messenger was a native Canadian product, while such cars as the McLaughlin Buick, Chevrolet, Pontiac, and Oakland were American makes put together in Oshawa itself. Also on display are examples of Dodge and Ford (assembled at Windsor, Ontario), Reo (St Catherine's, Ontario), Star, Durant, Willys-Knight and Overland (Toronto), and Gray-Dort (Chatham, Ontario). An American rarity is the 1912 Atlas.

Prince Edward Island
Car Life Antique Car Museum,
Bonshaw,
Prince Edward Island
Open every day May 17–October 10 9.00–21.00
Mr Newton Mackay's Car Life Museum includes

National V12, 1917. Courtesy Western Canadian Pioneer Museum, Wetaskiwin, Alberta, Canada

upwards of a dozen cars and trucks, as well as horsedrawn carriages and farm machinery. The cars embrace a 1906 Maxwell, three Canadian-built McLaughlin Buicks of the 1920s and 1930s, Fords Model T and A, 1928 Dodge, and a Willys and Pontiac of 1931. There is a 1916 Federal fire truck.

Saskatchewan
Western Development Museum,
1839 11th Street West,
Saskatoon,
Saskatchewan
Open every day 9.00–21.00 (summer)
The Western Development Museum is dedicated to the preservation of the way of life of the people who pioneered the Great Plains of western Canada. It has one of the finest collections devoted to agriculture in North America – agricultural machinery, house furnishings, reconstructed buildings, a fire engine, horse bus, locomotive and early aeroplane; also motor cars, of which there are no less than 250, around 75 being in working order. There are examples of the Canadian Russell, the IHC, Brush, Holsman, and Cadillac; Rauch & Lang electric, Studebaker, and Citroen halftrack. The last-named is a relic of Charles Bedaux' Arctic expedition of 1934. Smaller branches of the museum, without cars, are at North Battleford and Yorkton.

CHILE
*
Joachim Frewin Collection,
Santiago de Chile
Opening seasons and times not communicated
Mr Joachim Frewin has a small collection of about eight or nine cars, including a 1908 Renault, a Packard of the 1920s, an Auburn, and various Fords.

CZECHOSLOVAKIA
National Technical Museum,
Kostelni 42,
Prague 7
Open every day 10.00–17.00
The Hall of Transport in Czechoslovakia's National Technical Museum displays a fine collection of the nation's historic transportation relics–locomotives, aircraft, cars, motor cycles and bicycles. The oldest car on show is the 1897 Nesselsdorf, an 1899 racing car from the same factory, 1906, 1912 and 1924 Laurin-Klements and a 1906 Velox, a 1935 Wikov racing car, and a 1950 Aero-Minor. There are Tatras of 1899, 1924, 1930, and 1947. All these are of Czechoslovakian construction. Of the foreign cars, the most unusual are the very early 1912 Bugatti Type 13 and the 1938 Mercedes-Benz Grand Prix car of the three litre formula. The motor cycles include the 1893 Hildebrand und Wolfmuller and examples of Laurin-Klement, Jawa, Perun and Poustka.

Tatra six-wheeler. Courtesy Tatra Technical Museum, Koprivnice, Czechoslovakia

Tatra Technical Museum,
Koprivnice
Open every day 8.00–16.00
The Tatra works museum has an extremely fine
collection of cars and trucks, between 30 and 40
in number. The cars include most types
produced by the present concern or its
predecessors, ranging from a 1901 type B
Nesselsdorf to a 1950 Type 607 Tatra racing
machine. There are also more than 100 engines
on show.

A general view of the National Technical Museum, Prague. Courtesy National Technical Museum,
Prague, Czechoslovakia

DENMARK

Aalholm Automobil Museum,
Nysted, near Nykobing F.,
Lolland

Open every day June-mid October 10.00–18.00

The museum at Aalholm is an extremely large one for Scandinavia, with about 200 cars dating from between 1896 and 1930, propelled by gasoline, steam or electricity. They include a 1902 Renault landaulet, a Rambler of the same year, a 1904 Cadillac, a 1906 Model N Ford, a fine 1906–7 Brasier and 1909–10 Delaunay-Belleville, a 1917 Stanley steamer, 1917 friction-drive Metz, 1914 Benz, 1932 Hispano-Suiza, and four Rolls-Royces. Visitors whose children are bored by cars can see an extensive model railway layout covering over 600 square yards. Furthermore, a full-sized railway with 1850 engine and rolling stock runs through one of the exhibition halls and down to a beach.

*

Danmarks Tekniske Museum,
Nordre Strandvej 27,
Helsingor

Open every day 10.00–17.00

Denmark's Museum of Science and Industry, a private institution, was founded in 1911, but its property was not exhibited until 1966, and then on a small scale. The items on view are naturally representative mostly of Danish industry. The most important of the 15 cars is the Hammel, attrributed to 1886, Denmark's oldest surviving motor vehicle. Here also is a product of the Dansk Automobil-og-Cykelfabrik dating from 1899, and made by H. C. Christiansen. The most recent cars shown are examples of the first Folkevogn and Volvo – the latter, of course, being from Sweden. Other foreign cars include a 1906 Delaunay-Belleville used by the Danish royal family, a 1912 Swift, and a rare 1922 Szawe from Germany with Neumann-Neander bodywork. Two

Danish-built motor cycles on display are the 1905 Elleham and the Nimbus of 1922. There are no fewer than four Danish aeroplanes from the pre-1914 period.

Det Jyske Automobilmuseum,
Gjern,
near Silkeborg

Open every day June to mid-August 13.00–18.00
April–November Saturdays 13.00–18.00
April–November Sundays 10.00–18.00

There are some 60 vehicles in Mr Aage Louring's museum, dating from between 1913 and 1957, most of them American. Among the most unusual are a Type 51 Fiat of 1916, a 1932 V12 Auburn, 1929 Kissel, 1928 Jordan and 1922 Hansa-Lloyd fire truck.

* *

Egeskovmuseet,
Egeskov,
near Odense

Open every day summer months to end September 10.00–18.00

The motor museum in the castle at Egeskov has a couple of dozen vehicles on show, including 1905 and 1912 Renaults, a Mack truck of 1915, and a 1912 Wanderer. A real rarity is the much more recent Rovin, a French economy car dating from 1946. There are also three aircraft from the Second World War.

* *

Trafik-Historisk-Museum,
Petershvile,
near Helsingor

Open every day in summer months 10.00–20.00

Around 40 cars are on show at Petershvile, embracing contrasts as far apart as the 1907 Cyclonette three-wheeler and the L29 front wheel drive Cord. There are also a Type 40 Bugatti and a V12 Cadillac. The cars on show belong to members of the Dansk Veteranbil Klub.

Hotchkiss, 1926. Courtesy Det Jyske Automobilmuseum, Gjern, Denmark

Renault, 1898. Courtesy Autobiographie Renault, Paris, France

FRANCE

Autobiographie Renault,
Avenue des Champs Elysées,
Paris
Open every day
The Autobiographie Renault is that company's museum, situated in their showrooms in the Champs Elysées. It is one of the finest one-make collections in Europe, displaying 20 vehicles from 1898 to 1966. They take in the original 1898 *voiturette* and one of 1901, a 1902 Paris–Vienna racing car, a 1921 tourer of unRenault-like sporting aspect, a charming 1922 KJ sedan, the luxury Reinastella of 1932, and from the post-Second World War era, the 1956 experimental gas turbine machine Etoile Filante and a 1966 Alpine.

Autorama Delagrange,
D 94,
Yerres,
Essonne
Open every day except Sunday 14.00–19.00
In their museum at Yerres, the Baron de Gourgaud and Monsieur Rousseau have gathered together about 70 cars, mainly of the 1920s. Classic cars from this decade and the 1930s predominate, as witness the three Voisins (C7, C14 and C23), the four Bugattis (Types 44, 43A, and 57C), the three Talbots, the three Lorraine-Dietrichs, two Delages, two Hispano-Suizas, and two Delahayes. From foreign countries, there are an AK Minerva of 1932 and (oddly) a 1931 V16 Cadillac. Finally, there are half a dozen horsedrawn carriages.

A general view, Autobiographie Renault, Paris, France

Renault Paris-Vienna racing car, 1902. Courtesy Autobiographie Renault, Paris, France

Renault ambulance, 1918. Courtesy Autorama Delagrange, Yerres, France

Conservatoire National des Arts et Métiers,
292 rue Saint-Martin,
Paris 3
Open every day except Monday
Tuesday–Saturday 13.30–17.30
Sunday 10.00–17.00
The road transport collection of the
Conservatoire National, though comparatively
small, is one of the two or three most
important in France, possessing as it does an
almost unparalleled display of crucially
important vehicles from the earliest times. Apart
from horsedrawn vehicles and bicycles and a
number of historic engines, gearboxes,
carburettors and means of ignition, here are
Cugnot's steam tractor of 1771 (the grandfather
of them all), Amédée Bollée's steam carriage
'L'Obéissante' of 1873, the De Dion–Bouton
steam tricycle of 1885 and Serpollet's of 1888, a
Millet motor cycle of 1893, one of the first De
Dion motor tricycles (1895), and a 1903 racing
steamer by Serpollet. One oddity is the Marcel
Leyat airscrew-propelled car of 1920.

Museon di Rodo,
3 bis, Route de Nîmes,
Uzès,
Gard
Open every day Easter–October 10.00–12.00,
15.00–19.00
Monsieur Girod-Eymery's collection, one of the
finest in the south of France, aims at bringing to
life the history of the motor car (and also of the
railway, since there is a notable display covering
this field of transportation, too). In addition, there
are 40 motor cycles and bicycles, as well as
models, posters, etc. Like many other collections,
the items on show change frequently, but the 45
cars have included an 1897 Peugeot, 1898
Clement-De Dion, 1904 Le Métais, 1907 Renault,
an Alcyon of the same year, a 1923 De Dion
Bouton, 1926 Amilcar CGS, 1929 $4\frac{1}{2}$ Litre Bentley,
a Bugatti Type 13 of 1912 and a 1935 Type 57, and
a 1939 $4\frac{1}{4}$ Litre Bentley with formal bodywork
embellished with carriage lamps. The museum is
due to be moved to larger premises at the railway
station (Pont de Charrettes).

De Dion Bouton, 1900. Courtesy Museon di Rodo, Uzès, France

Musée de l'Automobile de Rochetaillée-sur-Saône,
Château de Rochetaillée-sur-Saône,
Rhône
Open every day
March 15 – October 9.00 – 12.00, 14.00 – 19.00
November – March 14 10.00 – 12.00, 14.00 – 18.00
The collection of Henri Malartre, one of the finest
in France, aims at including the best vehicles of
every class. Its emphasis is on pre-First World
War machines, on local products of the Lyon
region, renowned for its automotive industry, and
on mechanical oddities, though all sorts are
represented. There are something like 160 cars,
motor cycles, fire trucks and bicycles; over 2,000
models; and a display of more than 700 posters,
photographs, and car parts and accessories that
is claimed to be unique in Europe. It is possible
to mention only some of the highlights. Among
the very early machinery are an 1895 Rochet-
Schneider, a Peugeot of the same year, an 1898
Gobron-Brillié with opposed-piston engine,
a 1902 Motobloc-Schaudel with monobloc engine
and unit construction of engine and gearbox, a
De Dion tricycle of 1897, 1896 Leon Bollée, 1897

Hugot and Vallée, 1894 Benz, 1896 Laspougeas,
and the daddy of them all, the Secretant steamer
of 1890. From later times come the sports cars:
the 1925 Th. Schneider; the Lorraine-Dietrich, also
1925; the Le Mans-type Darl'Mat of 1937
(Peugeot-based); the 1951 Talbot Lago; and the
1955 Mercedes-Benz 300SL. Outstanding among
more touring machinery of the period are the
great 40CV Renault of 1923, the 1926 Slim-Pilain,
the odd 1932 Voisin, the eight-cylinder Derby of
1934, and the V12 Hispano-Suiza of the same year.
Monsieur Malartre's collection is really strong in
pure racing machines, such as the 1908
Sizaire-Naudin, Rolland-Pilains of 1909 and 1923,
Type 35B Bugatti, 1949 Talbot Lago, 1952 and
1954 Gordinis, and the Ferrari and Osca of 1953.
Here, too, are the peculiar: the 1926 Sizaire Frères
and Monotrace, the prototype 2CV Citroen of 1936,
and the 1948 J. P. Wimille. The motor-cycle
enthusiast can see such machines as the 1899
Georges Richard and an early scooter, the 1922
Skootamota. At the other extreme is the
four-cylinder F.N. of 1904, the 1903 Swiss Dufaux,
and the 1927 Brough Superior.

Scotte, 1892. Courtesy Musée de l'Automobile, Rochetaillée-sur-Saône, France

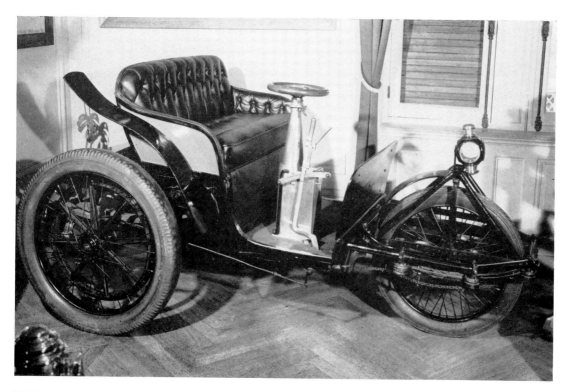

Milde, 1900. Courtesy Musée de l'Automobile, Rochetaillée-sur-Saône, France

Léon Bollée, 1912. Courtesy Musée de l'Automobile, Rochetaillée-sur-Saône, France

Musée de l'Abbatiale,
Le Bec-Helouin 27,
Eure
Open April–November every day except Tuesday
Monsieur Chassaing de Borredon's collection of
30 cars, all restored, includes no fewer than five
Bugattis (Types 23, 40, 40A, 44, and 57C); also an
1899 De Dion tricycle, 1937 Amilcar Compound,
1938 Peugeot Darl'Mat, and examples of Mathis,
Delage, Hispano-Suiza, Talbot, Hotchkiss,
Salmson, and Ferrari. Possibly the rarest vehicle
is a Simca-Gordini of 1937.

Musée de la Moto et du Velo,
Lunéville
Meurthe-et-Moselle
Open every day
This museum contains about 150 machines,
comprising 90 motor cycles (of which two-thirds
are pre-1914), and 60 bicycles and tricycles. All
are in restored condition.

* * * *

Musée de Briare,
RN 7,
Briare, Loiret
Open every day July–August
9.00–12.00, 15.00–19.00 September–June,
Saturday and Sunday only 9.00–12.00, 15.00–19.00
Some former lime-kilns provide a home for
Monsieur Broual's important collection on the
RN 7, convenient for travellers between Paris and
Nice. In cavernous surroundings, relieved by
accessories and posters, are an 1895
Panhard-Levassor, a 1906 Rochet-Schneider, a
Phénix (undated) made by the firm that was more
widely known for engines, an odd 1920 flat-twin
Sphinx, a 1925 Sizaire Frères, one of the last
Georges-Irat, from 1938, a 1953
Hotchkiss-Grégoire, and probably rarest of all, a
1905 Chameroy. Among all this unusual native
machinery, to a total of about 50, is a 1955
British Kieft of the 500 cc. Formula Three.

Bugatti Type 23, 1920. Courtesy Musée Automobile de l'Abbatiale, Le Bec-Helouin, France

Simca-Gordini, 1937. Courtesy Musée Automobile de l'Abbatiale, Le Bec-Hellouin, France

Talbot, 1937. Courtesy Musée Automobile de l'Abbatiale, Le Bec-Hellouin, France

Berliet Museum,
Automobiles M. Berliet,
Vénissieux,
Rhône
Open every day except Saturday and Sunday
8.00–17.00, except lunchtime
The Berliet company's magnificent collection of
early products is housed in their factory. The 20
vehicles owned include no fewer than three from
the nineteenth century: *voiturettes* of 1895 and
1897, and an 1897 victoria. There is the chassis of
a Targa Bologna racing car of 1906, and six cars
from the stately Edwardian age: three of 1908;
three of 1911. From the twenties is one passenger
car only: a 1921 touring machine. Commercial
and public service vehicles include a 1911 fire
engine, trucks of 1913 and 1914 and a
charcoal-gas-engined vehicle of 1941, and a 1918
bus. Berliet have always been interested in
'go-anywhere' vehicles, illustrated here by a 1926
machine intended for Sahara desert use, and a
Gazelle of 1959.

Musée d'Automobiles de Normandie,
D 6,
Clères
Open every day 8.30–20.00
Monsieur Jackie Pichon's museum at Clères is
one of the best known to British tourists, being
close to the Channel ports. Attached to an inn,
the Cheval Noir, it is also one with an
exceptionally attractive ambience. The collection
numbers about 40 and is an important one, very
well laid out. Its notable cars include an
exceedingly early Panhard-Levassor and
Peugeot, of 1893 and 1894 respectively, the odd
1900 Bolide and 1900 Goessant (a local breed),
two pioneers of their particular makes (a 1905
DFP and a 1906 Delage single-cylinder), a
delightful sporting Grégoire of 1910, three more
rarities in the shape of the 1920 Suère (a V8 of
less than a litre's capacity), the weird Monotrace
(a two-wheeled compromise between motor-cycle
and car), the 1923 three-cylinder Lafite, and
two unique vehicles: George Eyston's
record-breaking Panhard-Levassor of 1932, and
the 1948 CTA-Arsenal.

Berliet army lorry, 1914. Courtesy Berliet Museum, Vénissieux, France

Musée Automobile de Lourdes,
Esplanade du Paradis,
Lourdes
Open every day 9.00–21.00
This museum in the centre of Lourdes contains about 60 vehicles of all kinds, and a large collection of motor cycles, engines, parts, accessories and posters. It is associated with the Musée de l'Automobile du Mans (*q.v.*), with which it exchanges exhibits. On show are a three-wheeled De Montais steamer of 1882, an extremely early Panhard-Levassor (1890), and such rarities as the 1902 Luc Court, 1903 Mieusset, 1923 Goutte d'Eau, 1927 Turcat-Méry, 1929 record-breaking Panhard, 1931 Bucciali, and a Le Mans-type Simca Gordini that ran in the 1937 Le Mans 24 Hours Race.

Musée d'Automobiles du Forez,
D 105,
Sury-le-Comtal,
Loire
Open every day July–August 9.00–12.00, 15.00–19.00
Rest of year weekends only 9.00–12.00, 15.00–19.00
Monsieur Jacques Lefranc's collection amounts to around 40 cars, and includes machines rarely seen in France, let alone elsewhere. Among them are a 1923 MASE made in Saint-Etienne, a fine six-cylinder Germain of 1909 from Belgium, 1910 Motobloc, La Croix de la Ville three-wheeler, one of the great 50CV Delaunay-Bellevilles of 1914, a six-cylinder 1907 Minerva, and the 'Tank' model aerodynamic Chenard-Walcker of 1928. There are also a number of motor cycles, including a four-cylinder Henderson.

Musée Automobile de Bretagne,
Route de Fougères,
Rennes,
Ille-et-Vilaine
Open every day except Tuesday 9.00–19.00
Monsieur Louis Desbordes' collection includes motor cycles and scooters as well as cars, of which about 70 are on display. The most notable, for reasons of rarity or distinction, are the 1905 Barre, two very sporting 1908 Grégoires, a Ballot-engined Philos of 1910, a fine Lorraine-Dietrich torpedo of the same year, a 1912 Suère, 1927 Brasier (one of the last of the breed), and an Amilcar Compound of 1936.

Musée de l'Automobile du Mans,
Circuit Permanent de la Sarthe,
Le Mans,
Sarthe
Open every day Easter–October 9.00–12.00,
14.00–1900
November–Easter except Tuesday 9.00–12.00,
14.00–18.00
The museum at Le Mans is one of the biggest in France, with its more than 140 vehicles, of which most date from before 1920; but its historical significance is greater, on account of its high proportion of very early, very rare, or locally-built machines. In the former category are 1885 and 1887 De Dion-Bouton steamers, an 1888 Benz, one of the first front-engined Panhard-Levassors of 1892, an 1895 Delahaye, and an 1899 Renault. Among the local rarities are four Amédée Bollées of 1900, 1901, 1912 and 1916, and an 1897 Vallée. Seldom seen anywhere are the 1908 Delaugère-Clayette, 1909 Otto, 1914 Saiga, the airscrew-propelled Marcel Leyat of 1920, the Bobby-Alba, Soriano Pedroso and Françon of the same year, the 1924 Maurice Gendront, 1926 Guyot Spéciale, 1928 Alma Six and Oméga Six, 1936 16-cylinder Bucciali, 1938 Alphi, and the 1952 Socéma-Gregoire experimental turbine car. The Le Mans museum is associated with that at Lourdes (*q.v.*), and shares exhibits with it.

Musée de l'Automobile de Vatan,
Total Service Station,
RN 20,
Vatan,
Indre
Open every day
This small museum concentrates upon French cars, of which there are about a couple of dozen, mostly in excellent order, plus one Rolls-Royce and one Ford T. There are three Clément-Bayards, of 1906 (two) and 1910. A De Dion tricycle of 1902 can be seen, and also a fire truck of 1919. There is a 1902 Panhard-Levassor, and Delaunay-Bellevilles of 1908 and 1910. Less usual are the 1910 Bédélia, the two Le Zèbres of 1908 and 1910, the 1898 Delahaye, the 1908 Brouhot, 1906 Ariès, 1910 Turcat-Méry, 1912 Amédée Bollée, and – exceedingly rare – a 1913 Moreau Luxior.

Musée Bonnal-Renaulac,
80, rue Ferdinand-Buisson,
Bègles,
Gironde
Open every day 8.30–12.00, 13.00–17.30
This museum is situated in the Bonnal-Renaulac factory. Most of the 70 or 80 cars are unrestored, but they are a fascinating collection. An 1891 Peugeot (one of the very first) competes in interest with an equally primeval De Dietrich built in 1896 for the Czar of Russia, a 1901 Schaudel with unit construction of engine and gearbox, a 1912 Hispano-Suiza, and the star of the show, a 1914 Indianapolis Peugeot (four cylinders, 16 valves, two overhead camshafts, and front wheel brakes). Other rarities include two Georges Roy of 1910 and 1924, and a 1911 Violette. There are several motor cycles, too.

Musée National de la Voiture et du Tourisme,
Château de Compiègne,
Oise
Open every day March–October 10.00–12.00, 14.00–17.00
November–February 10.00–12.00, 14.00–16.30
The museum at Compiègne, forming with the collection at the Conservatoire National (*q.v.*) the two state transport museums of France, is almost the latter's equal in terms of historical importance, since it includes such key vehicles as 'La

Mancelle', Amédée Bollée's steamer of 1878; an 1885 diligence by the same maker; an 1889 De Dion-Bouton steam dogcart; no fewer than two Panhard-Levassors of 1891, the firm's first year of production; an 1895 gasoline car by Amédée Bollée *fils*; and an 1895 De Dion tricycle and Léon Bollée *voiturette* – both also of the earliest possible vintage. Here, too, is Camille Jenatzy's famous electric record-breaker 'La Jamais Contente', and one of the Citroen halftracks that crossed Africa in 1924. In all, the museum has 27 motor vehicles, plus a fine collection of horsedrawn carriages.

Musée Automobile de Provence,
RN 7,
13 Orgon,
Vaucluse
Open every day except Tuesday
Pierre Dellière's collection numbers about 45 cars, of which the most interesting are probably the racing cars – the 1925 BNC, a Mauve, 1925 Amilcar G6, and 1927 Rosengart. Among the passenger cars, special note should be taken of the 1924 Villard three-wheeler (the front wheel both steering and driving), the 1923 MASE, two Peugeots (the Darl'Mat of 1937 and the Type 202 sports prototype of 1936), the 1924 aircooled SARA, and the 1914 Reyrol. The museum also contains motor cycles, tricycles and bicycles.

Amilcar G6, 1925. Courtesy Musée Automobile de Provence, Orgon, France

Benz, 1900. Courtesy Verkehrsmuseum, Dresden, German Democratic Republic

GERMAN DEMOCRATIC REPUBLIC

Verkehrsmuseum,
Augustusstrasse 1,
801 Dresden
Open weekdays except Mondays 9.30–17.00
Sundays 9.30–13.00

There are about thirty motor vehicles in this, the only museum including cars at present open in the German Democratic Republic. Since it is a state collection, German cars naturally predominate–they include a very early three-wheeled Benz, 1894 and 1899 examples of the same make, and a Mercedes-Knight and a Wanderer of about 1911. Competition cars are represented by the AWE racer of 1957, and commercial vehicles by a 1902 Daimler truck. An interesting foreigner is the 1904 Excelsior from Switzerland. There are also motor cycles. Since this is a general transport museum, it embraces all forms of transport by land, sea and air.

Wanderer, 1904, Courtesy Verkehrsmuseum, Dresden, German Democratic Republic

Excelsior, 1904: made under Oldsmobile licence. Courtesy Verkehrsmuseum, Dresden, German Democratic Republic

Zweitakt-Motorrad-Museum,
9382 Augustusburg/Erzgebirge
Open every day 8.00–12.00, 13.00–16.30
This museum is a specialized one devoted
entirely to the two-stroke motor cycle, most of
them from either Germany or Austria. The 50
machines on show include an 1894 Hildebrand
und Wolfmuller, a 1921 Golem, a DKW motor
attached to a pedal cycle, Stock, Puch and
Zundapp, and racing models from BMW and
DKW/Auto-Union.

GERMAN FEDERAL REPUBLIC
Deutsches Vergaser Museum
Solex Vergaser,
Heidestrasse 52,
1 Berlin 21
Open every day 9.00–16.00
This is a museum of carburation, run by the
Deutsches Vergaser Gesellschaft on their
premises. It illustrates every method, from the
earliest instruments used by Siegfried Markus in
the 1870s to the most modern types.

Dunelt, 1927. Photo courtesy Zweitakt-Motorrad-Museum, Augustusburg, German Democratic Republic

A Markus carburettor, 1865. Courtesy Deutsches Vergaser Museum, Berlin, Germany

Daimler-Benz Museum,
Stuttgart-Untertürkheim

*Open every day except Sunday and public holidays
Monday–Friday 8.30–16.00 Saturday 8.30–13.00*
Although it is strictly a one-make (or rather
one-company) museum, the Daimler-Benz AG's
motor vehicle collection at Stuttgart is one of the
most important, largest and most comprehensive
in the world, because of the prominence of the
company that created it and because of the
former's efforts to perfect it. The present museum,
opened in 1961, has over 120 exhibits, displayed
on three floors. The ground floor virtually
illustrates the early history of the internal
combustion engine, since Gottlieb Daimler and
Karl Benz between them created the practical
motor vehicle. Here are a Daimler four-stroke and
a Benz two-stroke engine, both of 1882; the 1886
Daimler and Benz cars (the latter in replica form);
the 1889 Daimler 'steel wheel car' with vee-twin
engine; and a number of Daimler and Benz
products of the 1890s, including a fire engine and
a streetcar with Daimler engines. On the same
floor are examples of the first Mercedes-type

Daimler of 1902 that provided the basis of the
modern motor car; a magnificent 60 h.p.
Mercedes of 1903; a Knight sleeve-valve-engined
Mercedes of 1910 and touring Benzes of the same
era; a 28/95 h.p. Mercedes sports car;
supercharged Mercedes of the early postwar
years; and diesel commercial and passenger
vehicles. The first floor is devoted to aircraft and
aero engines, and to Mercedes-Benz cars dating
from the time of the merger between Daimler and
Benz in 1926. The latter take in fine examples of
the Type 540K and Grosser Mercedes-Benz of the
1920s and 1930s. On the second floor is an
unparalleled display of the companies' racing
cars, from the 1906 Grand Prix Mercedes through
the 1911 200 h.p. Benz and the 1914 Grand
Prix-winning Mercedes to the S-type sports car of
1927 (a model also used for racing), the
world-beating Grand Prix Mercedes-Benz of the
1930s (750 kg. and three litre formulas), and the
record-breakers of the same decade. Here, too,
is the 1954 Grand Prix car which carried on its
predecessors' winning tradition. A recent
acquisition is an 1899 Daimler racing car.

General view in the Daimler-Benz Museum, showing (foreground) the 1954–5 Formula I

Exterior of the Daimler-Benz Museum. Courtesy Daimler-Benz Museum, Stuttgart

General view in the Daimler-Benz Museum. Courtesy Daimler-Benz Museum, Stuttgart

Deutsches Zweiradmuseum,
Deutschordensschloss,
Neckarsulm
Open every day 9.00–12.00, 13.30–17.00
Germany's foremost motor cycle and bicycle museum, housed in a medieval castle, contains about 150 machines.

MAN-Museum,
Heinrich-von-Buz-Strasse 28,
Augsburg
Open weekdays 7.30–16.00 Sundays 10.00–13.00
The museum of the Maschinenfabrik Augsburg-Nurnberg AG, otherwise MAN, is devoted very largely, though not entirely, to the development of the diesel engine, from Rudolf Diesel's experimental unit of 1893 up to recent times. In this lies its interest to the motorist.

Klockner-Humboldt-Deutz AG Engine Museum,
Deutz-Mulheimer Strasse,
Koln-Deutz
Open Monday to Friday 9.00–17.00
This is a museum of stationary engines only, but since Nikolaus August Otto, who made the four-stroke principle work in internal-combustion engines, was one of the founders of the firm, the collection is of fundamental importance in the history of the motor vehicle. Here is seen a Lenoir gas engine, an Otto & Langen engine of 1867, and (the prize of the collection) a prototype four-stroke gas engine built by the company in 1876. One of 1877 is shown working. There is also a diesel engine of 1898, and exhibits showing the development of this type.

Otto's engine of 1876. Courtesy Klockner-Humboldt-Deutz AG Engine Museum, Cologne, German Federal Republic

Early diesel engines (left to right): 1893–5; 1898; the oldest two-cylinder engine (1898); and 1909.
Courtesy MAN-Museum, Augsburg, German Federal Republic

Rohr, 1928, a sectioned exhibit. Courtesy Deutsches Museum, Munich, German Federal Republic

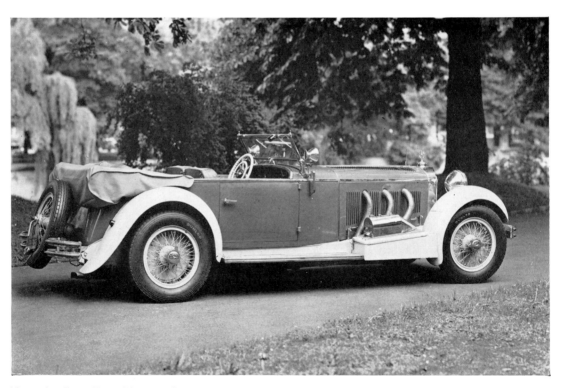

Mercedes-Benz Type SS, 1928. Courtesy Deutsches Museum, Munich, German Federal Republic

BMW Type 328 Mille Miglia, 1940. Courtesy BMW Museum, Munich, German Federal Republic

BMW Type 507, 1955–60. Courtesy BMW Museum, Munich, German Federal Republic

Deutsches Museum von Meisterwerken der Naturwisschenschaft und Technik, Museumsinsel 1, Munich

To be open every day 9.00–17.00

At the time of writing the new car hall of this important museum is closed to the public. Since it may be open by the time this book is published, a note follows of the more important car exhibits. These include the original 1886 Benz (that in the Daimler-Benz museum at Stuttgart – *q.v.* – being a replica), curiosities like the 1921 Slaby-Beringer electric, the rear-engined Rumpler, and the 1925 Hanomag economy car. At the other extreme are machines like the Alpine-type Audi of 1912, 1928 Röhr, a 1930 Type ADR Austro-Daimler, a 1939 Horch, and two Grand Prix cars – an Auto-Union of the 750 kg. formula, and a 1939 three litre formula Mercedes-Benz. Some early examples of their makes are the 1899 Mors, the 1900 Adler, and the 1904 Horch. There are, among the new acquisitions, a 1905 Victoria, a 1906 Mercedes, and a 1911 Adler.

BMW Museum, Lerchenauerstrasse 76, 8 Munich 13

Open Monday–Friday except public holidays 8.00–15.40

This collection, devoted to the famous cars, motor cycles, and aircraft engines of the company, contains about 20 cars. They include one of the 1940 aerodynamic Type 328 BMWs that won the Mille Miglia race of that year, examples of the original Austin Seven-based Dixi and of the later AM4, a BMW 315 and a 327/328 coupé, and a normal Type 328 sports model. From the postwar years are one of the splendid Type 507 sports cars, and a racing car of 1966 powered by a BMW two-litre engine.

Automuseum Nettelstedt, Rietkampstrasse, Nettelstedt 4991

Open Monday–Friday 11.00–19.00
Saturday and Sunday 10.00–19.00

This museum, which claims to be the biggest in Germany, has nearly 100 cars. The most notable are the 1898 Daimler four-cylinder, the 1912 and 1913 Hispano-Suizas, the latter being one of the Alfonso models, a Salmson racing *voiturette* of 1925, a Type 46 Bugatti and a 1912 Type 13 of the same make, an odd little Neumann-Neander of 1939, a Maybach W5 of 1925, two of the SW38 model from the same factory, a supercharged front wheel drive Alvis (an unusual sight in Germany), two supercharged Mercedes-Benz (one the rare Type 380, the other a Type SS), and an 1898 Seck (on the Benz system).

Auto-Museum L. L. Hillers, 2071 Tremsbüttel bei Bargteheide

Open every day April–November, 11.00–20.00
December–March, Sundays only 11.00–20.00

About 47 cars in this fine collection are fully restored and on show to the public. Naturally the emphasis is on German makes, such as Adler, Audi, Benz, BMW, Brennabor, Colibri, Cyklonette, DKW, Hanomag, Horch, Mercedes-Benz, Opel, Presto, Piccolo, Wanderer, Lloyd and NSU; but French, Italian and British makes are also represented in what is intended as a cross-section of the history of the motor car. It is unusual to see three Hanomags together anywhere; the Mercedes-Benz include a 500K of 1935; and the Opels an Opel-Darracq of 1900. At the time of writing there are also about 50 cars and 20 motor cycles awaiting restoration.

GREAT BRITAIN

Museum of British Transport, Clapham High Street, London, S.W.4

Open every day except Sunday, Good Friday, Christmas Day and Boxing Day 10.00–17.30

This magnificent collection, which at the time of writing is threatened with breaking up and dispersal to other centres, outdoes even that of the Science Museum (*q.v.*) in its scope and size. The accent is on public service transport–there are no passenger or commercial vehicles on show. Beside historic locomotives and railway coaches can be seen trams, trolleybuses, motor and horsedrawn buses, and models. The motor buses include a 1911 B-Type, 1919 K-Type, and an S-Type of 1920, among seven that belonged to the London General Omnibus Company.

Cheddar Motor Museum,
Cheddar,
Somerset
*Open every day except Christmas Day
10.00-dusk*
Most of the cars in the Cheddar Motor Museum are owned by members of the Veteran Car Club of Great Britain, including most of the more interesting ones. These embrace an 1899 Star, 1901 Locomobile steamer, 1902 De Dion Bouton, 1903 Thornycroft and White steamer, 1904 Renault, a 1905 Corre, a Buick and a Rover of 1906, a 1911 Swift and Garrad Speke, 1912 Buick and Ford, 1913 Enfield, a Morris and a Renault of 1914, and a 1915 Studebaker. An unusual post-First World War car is the 1919 Talbot. There are also a portable steam engine of 1883, a 1912 traction engine, and a number of motor cycles and bicycles. There are rarities among the former – a 1927 Federation, 1920 NUT, and 1923 Sun.

The City Museum,
Queens Road,
Bristol 8,
Somerset
Open every day except Sunday 10.00–17.30
The Department of Technology of the Bristol City Museum is devoted principally to material illustrating the industrial and transport history of the Bristol area. Not all the vehicles listed here are on show; their display awaits the erection of a new city museum. They include the famous Grenville steam carriage, built in 1875 at Newton Abbot and the oldest extant mechanically-propelled road vehicle in Britain; a locally-made Bristol car of 1906, a 1926 bus chassis and a 1953 truck from the same manufacturer; an 1898 Daimler; the second Morris built, dating from 1913; and a 1912 Dennis fire truck and a 1934 Scammell mechanical horse, both formerly used by the Great Western Railway.

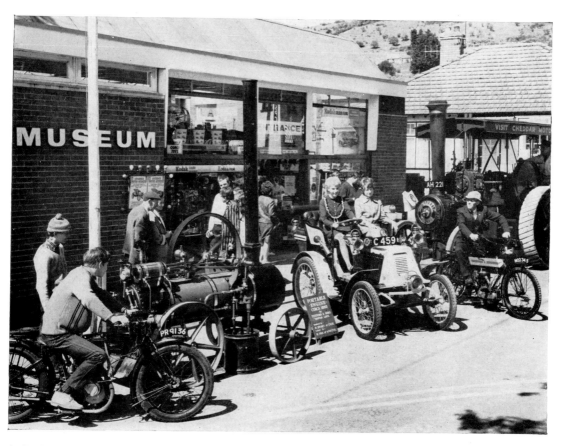

A display outside the Cheddar Motor Museum. Courtesy Cheddar Motor Museum, Cheddar, Somerset, England

A general view of the Cheddar Motor Museum. Courtesy Cheddar Motor Museum, Cheddar, Somerset, England

Grenville, 1875. Courtesy City Museum, Bristol, Somerset, England

Museum of Science and Industry,
Newhall Street,
Birmingham 3
Warwickshire
Open every day Weekdays 10.00 – 17.00 Saturdays
10.00 – 17.30 Sundays 14.00 – 17.30 First Wednesday
in month 10.00 – 21.00
The Transport Section houses about 30 cars of a remarkable range of rarity and noteworthiness, concentrating on Birmingham products. To be seen here are the monster Railton Mobil Special that held the World's Land Speed Record from 1947 to 1964, and a 200 h.p. 'Blitzen'-type Benz of 1912; at the other end of the scale in size if not interest are the experimental petrol-electric Lanchester of 1922, with friction-roller final drive and wooden body, chassis and suspension (and a 1901 10 h.p. model); a Castle Four of 1919 (rare anywhere and at any time); and a very early Star of 1898. About half of the exhibits (including the Benz and the 1901 Lanchester) are on loan. There are also a number of motor cycles.

Transport Museum,
High Street,
Kingston-upon-Hull,
Yorkshire
Open every day except Christmas Day and
Good Friday
Weekdays 10.00–17.00 Sundays 14.30–16.30
The Transport Museum at Hull covers every form of road vehicle from manual fire engines, sleighs and sedan chairs to horsedrawn carriages and coaches (an extremely fine collection), bicycles, motor cycles, tramcars and motor cars. The last-named include an 1898 Coventry Motette (the British version of the Léon Bollée), a De Dion Bouton quadricycle of 1899, an 1897 Panhard-Levassor, 1899 Daimler, 1900 Sturmey (a real rarity), a 1900 Cleveland electric, 1901 Marshall-Benz, and 1901 Gardner-Serpollet and White steamers. The motor cycles embrace a 1914 Rudge Multi, and a variety of lightweights: an Autowheel of 1919, a Grigg motor scooter of about 1923, and a Wall Autowheel attachment of 1914.

A general view of the Transport Section of the Birmingham Museum of Science and Industry, England

Montagu Motor Museum,
Beaulieu,
Brockenhurst,
Hampshire

Open every day except Christmas Day, April–October 10.00–18.00 November–March 10.00–17.00

The present Lord Montagu of Beaulieu founded the Montagu Motor Museum in 1952 as a memorial to his father, who was one of Britain's leading automotive pioneers. At first it consisted of a few vehicles only, displayed inside Palace House. Outbuildings were erected in 1956, when a couple of dozen cars could be seen; but within three years, a complex of new buildings housed about a hundred cars, the same amount of motor cycles and a number of commercial vehicles, bicycles, tricycles, horsedrawn vehicles, engines, models and components. Including as it does a great many extremely important exhibits on loan from other collections, the Montagu Motor Museum is not only the largest but also the most significant in Britain. The competition cars shown include 6C 1500 and 8C 2300 Alfa Romeos; 1908 Grand Prix and 1936 twin o.h.c. supercharged Austins; a 1957 BRM; the famous ERA 'Romulus'; the 1907 Coppa della Velocita Itala; a W196 Mercedes-Benz of 1954; a 1936 Riley works team car; a 1908 Tourist Trophy Thornycroft; and last but very far from least, no fewer than three holders of the World's Land Speed Record; the 1920 350 h.p. Sunbeam, the 1000 h.p. of 1927 from the same maker, and Sir Henry Segrave's 'Golden Arrow' of 1929. Less exciting, perhaps, but all rare, odd or exotic in some way are the 1935 Auburn speedster, 1925 19/70 Austro-Daimler, a twin-cylinder Benz of 1898, 1904 Brushmobile, Type 30 Bugatti of 1925, the 1901 Columbia electric supplied to Queen Alexandra, the elegant German Daimler of 1898, a fine 1903 De Dietrich, an Alfonso-model Hispano-Suiza, one of Field-Marshal Montgomery's Humber staff cars, the 1895 Knight (one of Britain's first cars), two Lanchesters of 1908 and 1912, the first Wolseley of 1895, a 1903 60 h.p. Mercedes, and an extreme eccentricity in the form of the 1896 Pennington.

At the time of writing, plans are in hand to turn the Montagu Motor Museum into the national transport museum, with new museum and library buildings, an exhibition arena, and new tourist facilities, supported by charitable trusts financed partly by British industry.

The Montagu Motor Museum, Beaulieu, Hampshire

Alfa Romeo, 1929. Courtesy Montagu Motor Museum, Beaulieu, Hampshire

Record breakers in the Montagu Motor Museum: 1929 Golden Arrow (left); 1927 1000 h.p.
Sunbeam (right). Courtesy Montagu Motor Museum, Beaulieu, Hampshire

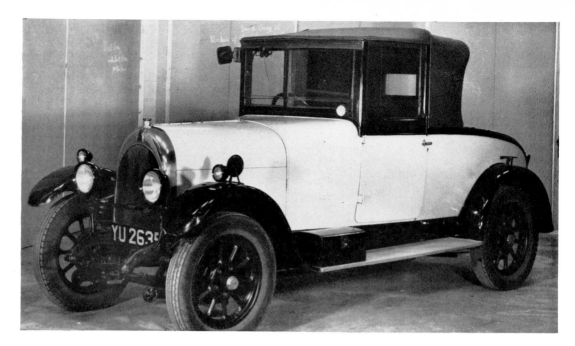

Bean, 1926. Courtesy Museum of Science and Industry, Birmingham, England

Benz 200 h.p., 1912. Courtesy Museum of Science and Industry, Birmingham, England

The Royal Mews,
Buckingham Palace,
London, S.W.1
Open Wednesday and Thursday 14.00–16.00
The Royal Mews at Buckingham Palace show
motor cars and horsedrawn carriages that have
belonged to the British Royal Family. There are
three of the former displayed, of which the most
interesting is the Daimler 'Royal Phaeton' made
for King Edward VII when Prince of Wales in
1900. Two other machines are being restored.

The Shuttleworth Collection,
Old Warden Aerodrome,
Biggleswade,
Bedfordshire
Open every day April–September
Weekdays 9.00–17.00
Saturday and Sunday 11.00–18.00
October–March every day 10.00-dusk
The Shuttleworth Trust was founded in memory
of Richard Shuttleworth, who was killed in the
Second World War and was a collector of early
aircraft and cars. His machines form the nucleus
of the present Shuttleworth Collection. Its most
important feature is its aircraft, which range from
the Frost Ornithopter of 1868 to a Jet Provost
trainer of 1962. Many of the aircraft on show are
originals, including a Bleriot of 1909, a 1910
Deperdussin, a 1912 Blackburn, First and Second
World War machines, and light aircraft from
between the wars. There are also several replicas
of early aircraft built for the film *Those Magnificent
Men in their Flying Machines*. Most are in flying
order, and can be seen in action on open
weekends. The cars on show in the hangars
include an 1897 Daimler, 1898 Panhard-Levassor,
1898 Benz, 1899 Mors, 1900 Marot-Gardon
quadricycle, 1901 Arrol-Johnston, 1901 Locomobile
steamer, 1902 Bébé Peugeot, 1903 De Dietrich
(probably the star of the collection), 1912
Crossley, 1913 Morris Oxford, and 1929 Alfa
Romeo. In addition, there are many motor cycles,
aero engines, bicycles, and horsedrawn carriages
to be seen.

Herbert Art Gallery & Museum,
Jordan Well,
Coventry,
Warwickshire
*Open every day except Christmas Day and
Good Friday*
Monday, Thursday, Friday, Saturday 10.00–18.00
Sunday, Tuesday, Wednesday 10.00–20.00
This important car collection is very much a local
one, restricted to products of the Coventry area,
which was the heart of the British road transport
industry from the days of the first bicycles. Of
between 50 and 60 cars, about a third are on
loan, and only a small portion is on show at any
one time. There is a very early Coventry product
in the shape of a Daimler of 1897–8, four other
Daimlers of 1906–26 including one of the
fabulous twelve-cylinder cars, some familiar
names (Humber, Morris, Rover, Riley, Standard,
Alvis) and some recherché ones – Crowden,
Stoneleigh, Maudslay (two of these rarities, of 1909
and 1910), Arden, Payne & Bates, and Crouch.

Trentham Motor Museum,
Trentham Gardens,
Stoke-on-Trent,
Staffordshire
Open every day March–October 12.00-dusk
At present this small collection comprises about
nine cars dating from between 1899 and the 1930s,
four fire engines, horsedrawn vehicles, bicycles
and weapons. The motor vehicles include a 1901
Darracq, 1909 FN, 1912 Rover, 1915 Peugeot, 1904
De Dion Bouton, 1912 Delahaye, 1909 Renault
van, and the odd 1907 Robinson with exhaust-
cooled engine.

Veteran and Vintage Car Museum,
Caister Castle,
Great Yarmouth
Open every day May–September 10.00–17.30
There are over 50 cars in this collection, as well
as motor cycles.

Nardi Danese racing car, 1947. Courtesy the Doune Collection, Doune Park, Perthshire, Scotland

The Doune Collection,
Doune Park,
Doune,
Perthshire.
Open every day 10.00–18.00
Lord Doune's private collection, newly opened to the public, consists of 27 cars at the time of writing. The most interesting are undoubtedly the 1929 and 1934 Maserati Grand Prix cars (the latter being ex-Whitney Straight and Prince Bira); no fewer than two of the very rare 8C2900B Alfa Romeos, one of 1935 and the other a 1938 Le Mans works car; the Nardi Danese racing car of 1947; and two Hispano-Suizas, one an H6B of 1924 and the other an unusual Type 26 of 1934, with 4½-litre Ballot engine.

Pembrokeshire Motor Museum,
Garrison Theatre,
Pembroke Dock,
Pembrokeshire
Open every day Easter–September from 10.00
Most of the exhibits in the Pembrokeshire Motor Museum are changed frequently, but at the time of writing the semi-permanent residents included Léon Bollées of 1896 and 1897, a 1904 Arielette (the only one known), 1911 AC Sociable, 1924 Three Litre Bentley, a very late Rolls Royce Silver Ghost of 1925, a 1927 Graham-Paige and a 1937 Lagonda Rapide. Also shown are bicycles and motor cycles from the 1880–1930 period.

AC Sociable, 1911. Courtesy Pembrokeshire Motor Museum, Pembrokeshire, Wales

Motor Cycle and Car Museum,
Stanford Hall,
near Rugby, Warwicks.
Open Easter – September
Thursdays, Saturdays and Sundays 14.30 – 18.00
Bank holidays 12.00 – 18.00
It is not widely known outside the Midlands that Standford Hall contains not only its famous collection of motor cycles, but also pictures, documents, antique furniture, costumes, kitchen utensils – and cars. There are now several of these, including an 1897 Hurtu and a 1920 Carden cyclecar. The motor cycles are, however, the main attraction; indeed Stanford Hall now has one of the most important collections in the world.

Royal Scottish Museum,
Chambers Street,
Edinburgh 1
Midlothian
Open every day except Christmas Day and New Year's Day
Monday – Saturday 10.00 – 17.00 Sunday 14.00 – 17.00
The Hall of Power in this museum contains a Scottish-built Albion dogcart of 1900; the second of the breed built. There are also various engines on show. In the cellar are several more cars: a Léon Bollée of 1896, an Arnold-Benz (British-built) of a year later, and a Locomobile steamer of 1900; also a number of motor cycles, the most important of which is the 1895 Holden with flat-four engine. Here, too, there are engines and bicyles.

Locomobile, ca. 1900. Courtesy Royal Scottish Museum, Edinburgh, Scotland

Albion, 1900. Courtesy Royal Scottish Museum, Edinburgh, Scotland

Museum of Transport,
25 Albert Drive,
Glasgow,
Renfrewshire
Open weekdays 10.00–17.00 Sundays 14.00–17.00
In addition to cars, the Glasgow Museum of
Transport contains collections of tramcars,
bicycles, horsedrawn vehicles, locomotives and
models. The motor vehicles number between 20
and 30, of which (fittingly) well over half are of
Scottish origin. They include Argylls from 1900,
1907, 1910, 1913 and 1927; Albions from 1900, 1904,
1910, 1918 and 1919; Arrol-Johnstons of 1901, 1912,
1920 and 1922; and a Beardmore and a Galloway
from 1924. There are also a 1929 $4\frac{1}{2}$ Litre Bentley,
a 1914 Th. Schneider, an 1898 Benz, and one
unique exhibit: the chassis from one of Sir
Goldsworthy Gurney's steam road carriages of the
early 19th century.

*

The Transport Museum,
Witham Street,
Belfast,
Northern Ireland
Open every day 9.00–16.00
This museum concentrates mainly upon railway
exhibits, but there are also many models, about
20 horsedrawn carriages, 10 motor cycles, six fire
trucks, and 20 motor cars. Probably the most
interesting of the latter are the vehicles of Irish
origin, notably the 1908 Chambers.

Murray's Motor Cycle Museum,
The Bungalow,
Snaefell,
Isle of Man
Open every day May–September 10.00–18.00
Murray's Motor Cycle Museum, situated on the
Tourist Trophy course, contains upwards of 130
machines dating from between 1901 and 1940. Its
home being the island where the famous Tourist
Trophy races are held, this museum naturally
attracts great interest, especially as it includes a
number of TT machines. Among them is a 1904
works Minerva. There are many engines; also
historic bicycles, a stage coach, weapons, musical
boxes, musical instruments and clocks.

Argyll, 1907. Courtesy Museum of Transport, Glasgow, Scotland

Albion van, 1910. Courtesy Museum of Transport, Glasgow, Scotland

Manx Motor Museum,
Crosby,
Isle of Man
Open every day May 21–September 21
Weekdays 10.00–17.00, Sundays 14.00–17.00
This collection of 20 to 30 vehicles, horsedrawn
and mechanically propelled, which ranges over
the century 1850–1950, starts chronologically with
a horsedrawn fire engine and ends with cars that
include several Bentleys of the 1920s.

Myreton Motor Museum,
near Aberlady,
East Lothian
Also at Dunbar (horsedrawn vehicles)
Open every day summer months 10.00–18.00
The 35 cars in this Scottish collection have
become more famous than do most museum
vehicles because of the participation of some in
the television series *Dr Finlay's Case Book*. The
exhibits include a 1924 Alvis (one of the oldest
survivors), a Phantom 1 Rolls Royce, a very early
Three Litre Bentley and a 1930 Speed Six and
1931 Eight Litre of the same make, 1930 Delage,
1927 Darracq and Galloway, several MGs, two
Lagondas, a British Salmson, and a Citroen
Kégresse half-track. There are a number of motor
cycles and bicylces.

Morris Oxford, 1926. Courtesy Myreton Motor
Museum, East Lothian, Scotland

Bentley Four Litre, 1931. Courtesy Manx Motor Museum, Isle of Man

The Science Museum,
South Kensington,
London, S.W.7
*Open every day except Christmas Day and Good
Friday. Monday–Saturday 10.00–18.00
Sunday 14.30–18.00*

The Road Transport Collection of the Science
Museum is Britain's most important state
transport museum, since as might be expected,
it owns most of the more significant survivors
from the early days of the British motor industry.
Some of these are on loan to other museums
(Montagu Motor Museum, *q.v.*). However, among
the cars to be seen at South Kensington are the
second Lanchester, made in 1896; the oldest
surviving Rolls-Royce (1904) and one of the first
Silver Ghosts (1909); and the Rover gas turbine
car of 1954 (the world's first). The Collection sets
out to show the history of the world's transport,
so here, too, are a Benz of 1888–the oldest car in
Britain–an 1894 Panhard-Levassor which
completed Britain's first cross-country car trip in
the following year, and a Wankel-engined NSU
from 1966. Needless to say, the Collection houses
motor cycles, bicycles, horsedrawn carriages and
railway relics in profusion. Its exhibits are housed
in the magnificent new Transport Galleries of the
museum.

Bentley Three Litre, 1924. Courtesy Science
Museum, London

Lanchester, 1896. Courtesy Science Museum, London

A general view of the Science Museum, London. On the left is the 1888 Benz. Courtesy Science Museum, London

Morgan, 1913. Courtesy Science Museum, London

HOLLAND

National Automobile Museum,
Veursestraatweg 280,
Leidschendam
Open every day 9.00–18.00
Most of the cars that were to be seen in the
now-defunct National Museum van die Automobiel
at Driebergen were sold to this new museum,
where about 90 vehicles are on show. The heir
to Mr Riemer's magnificent collection thus now
becomes Holland's foremost motor museum. The
cars include examples of Benz (1894), Darracq,
FN, Opel (1910), Gregoire (1909), Panhard-
Levassor, Spyker (1906 and 1916), De Dion
Bouton, Hispano Suiza, Voisin (1930),
Isotta-Fraschini (1925), Marmon (1930), and
Mercedes-Benz. Surprisingly, beside these cars
is a 1924 racing AC, as used at Brooklands.
There are six Rolls Royces and five Bugattis.
Among the oddities are the Scott Sociable, the
Cyklonette, and the Hansa-Lloyd electric. Also
exhibited are 30 motor cycles and 15 horsedrawn
carriages.

FN motor cycle, 1920 (foreground); FN car, 1900 (background). Courtesy National Automobile Museum,
Leidschendam, Holland

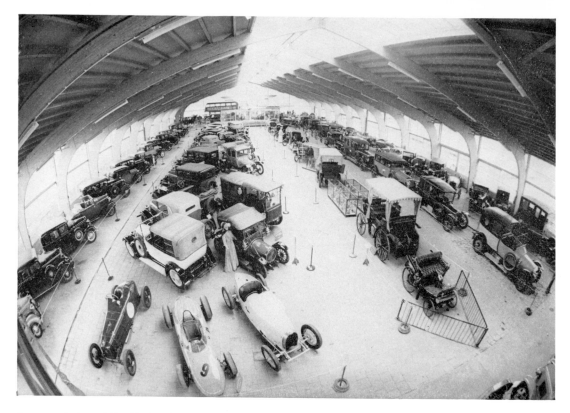

A general view of the National Automobile Museum. Courtesy National Automobile Museum, Leidschendam, Holland

Benz, 1894. Courtesy National Automobile Museum, Leidschendam, Holland

HUNGARY

Automuzeum Haris Testverek,
Moricz Zsigmond korter 12.
Budapest XI
Open every day 15.00 – 19.00
This private collection, run by the brothers Lajos
and Otto Haris, contains a dozen cars and motor
cycles and a large number of models. The former
are important because they include early
Hungarian machines such as the 1898, 1900 and
1904 Aurore, and an 1897 Ganz–De Dion tricycle.
Among the motor cycles are the 1893 Csonka-J,
1894 Ganz, and 1899 Aurore. Another two-wheeler
is a 1910 Wanderer.

Kozlekedesi Muzeum,
Varosligeti korut II,
Budapest XIV
*Open every day except Mondays and Fridays
10.00 – 18.00*
This, the Hungarian Communications Museum,
covers all means of transportation, though most
of the collection is devoted to railways and
steamships. The cars include many models, but
there are specimens of actual vehicles as well,
some from the pre-1914 period.

Aurore, 1900. Courtesy Auto Muzeum Haris
Testverek, Budapest, Hungary

Csonka, 1893. Courtesy Auto Muzeum Haris Testverek, Budapest, Hungary

A general view of the Museo dell'Automobile. Courtesy Museo dell'Automobile Carlo Biscaretti di Ruffia, Turin, Italy

ITALY

Museo Nazionale della Scienza e della Tecnica
  Leonardo da Vinci,
Via San Vittore 21,
Milan
Open every day
Although the Museo dell'Automobile in Turin
(*q.v.*) has the biggest public collection of cars in
Italy, the national transport collection, part of the
science museum in Milan, has an important
display of vehicles, ranging from horsedrawn
carriages, bicycles and motor cycles to several
cars, among them a Léon Bollée of 1896, a Bianchi
of around 1903, a 1923 San Giusto, a P2 Grand
Prix Alfa Romeo of 1924, a Fiat 509, two Isotta-
Fraschinis (an 8B of the early 1930s and one of the
few 8C Monterosas built, of 1947), and a Fiat gas
turbine car of 1954.

Museo dell' Automobile Carlo Biscaretti di Ruffia,
Corso Unita d'Italia 40,
Turin
*Open every day except Monday April–November 15
9.30–12.30, 15.00–19.00*
November 16–March 10.00–12.30, 15.00–17.30
Before the Second World War, the inspiration of
Count Carlo Biscaretti di Ruffia led to the
foundation of a motor museum in Turin, home of
the Italian motor industry. It was established at the
Municipal Stadium, with Biscaretti as Curator.
By 1956 the collection had outgrown these modest
premises, and the industry decided to provide a
more fitting home for it. 1960 saw the opening of
the present magnificent modern building, the
most impressive of its kind in the world. Aside
from imaginative displays illustrating the rubber
and gasoline industries, bodywork, and the
motor clubs, there are displays of engines,
carburation and ignition, a number of motor
cycles and bicycles, and between 250 and 300
cars and chassis. Picking out a few from among
the most notable of the former, and taking
competition cars first, we find Alfa Romeo P2 and
'Alfetta' Type 158; the 1951 Formula I Ferrari; 1907
Grand Prix Itala (and the 40 h.p. touring model of
the same year that won the Peking-Paris Trial);
1957 Maserati 250F; Mercedes-Benz W196;
Maserati Tipo 26B of 1928; and a gaggle of Italian
record-breakers such as the Monaco-Trossi (1935),
Nardi-Monaco (1932), Nibbio (1935), and Tarf

(1948). The pioneer vehicles are less exciting but
historically of the first importance: such are the
1854 Bordino and 1891 Pecori steamers, 1896
Bernardi (or Miari & Giusti), the 1894 Peugeot,
1893 Benz and 1899 Renault. The significant
touring cars include a 1912 Tipo Zero Fiat and the
Tipo 8 Isotta-Fraschini of 1920. If rarity (or oddity)
is the criterion, then such machines as the 1912
Aquila-Italiana, 1901 Ceirano, 1903 Florentia, the
pre-1914 Isotta-Fraschinis, 1908 Legnano, 1904
Marchand, 1902 Minutoli-Millo (the only one built),
1899 Prinetti & Stucchi, 1909 STAE electric, 1923
Temperino, 1911 Victrix and 1954 Fiat experimental
turbine car deserve attention.

JAPAN

Museum of Transportation,
25 Kanda-Sudacho, 1-chome,
Chiyoda-ku,
Tokyo
Open every day except Monday 9.30–17.00
The Museum of Transportation in Tokyo started
life as a railway museum, so it has few motor
vehicles. These include an air-cooled Franklin of
1931, a Model T Ford bus (of the type imported
after the 1923 earthquake, when every tramcar in
the city was destroyed), and a Datsun Model 15 of
1936, made by the Nissan Motor Company.

Datsun, 1936. Courtesy Museum of Transportation,
Tokyo, Japan

Model T Ford bus, 1923. Courtesy Museum of Transportation, Tokyo, Japan

NEW ZEALAND

Southward Museum,
Lower Hutt,
Wellington
Open Saturday and Sunday afternoons only
Mr L. B. Southward's collection has some true
rarities among the 35 or so cars on show; among
them are an 1897 Lux, a Tourist Trophy-type Rover
of 1907, an overhead-camshaft Maudslay of 1913,
and a 1939 Grand Prix Maserati. There are also
examples of 1900 De Dion Bouton, 1904 Wolseley,
and 1920 Stanley and 1907 White Steamers. In
contrast, here too are three recent racing cars:
a 1948 4CLT Maserati; a Ferrari; and a 250F
Maserati. The museum has about 100 cars and 20
motor cycles, but only a proportion are on display
at any one time. Beside them are no fewer than
eight fire engines.

Museum of Transport and Technology,
Western Springs,
Auckland
Open every day 10.00–17.00
Some exceptionally interesting vehicles among the
30-odd in this collection are the 1908 International
Auto Buggy, the Duo cyclecar of 1912, and a 1914
Renault with charabanc body. The museum
workshops are used by the Auckland Veteran &
Vintage Car Club to restore members' cars.

Yaldhurst Transport Museum,
School Road,
Yaldhurst,
Christchurch
Open every weekend and public holidays 10.00–17.00
The Yaldhurst Transport Museum, as its name
suggests, includes historic transportation of many
types. The motor vehicles, some owned by the
museum and some by the New Zealand Veteran
Car Club, embrace a 1903 Milwaukee and 1904
Orient Buckboard from America, a 1908 Daimler,
1910 Renault, 1913 Siddeley-Deasy, a 1914 Unic,
and many machines of the nineteen-twenties.
There is a 1924 Leyland fire engine, many motor
cycles and bicycles, and a fine collection of
horsedrawn vehicles.

NORWAY

Norsk Teknisk Museum,
Fyrstikkalleen 1, Oslo 6
Open every day except public holidays
Weekdays 10.00–16.00 Sundays 10.00–17.00
Norway's museum of science and industry has
among its transportation exhibits aeroplanes,
horsedrawn coaches, bicycles, motor cycles, and
cars. The 20 last-named include an 1895 Benz,
(the first car to come to Norway), a 1900
Locomobile steamer, 1903 Oldsmobile, 1910
Panhard-Levassor, and 1913 Minerva; but more
interesting because unusual are the
Lohner-Porsche electric of 1900, the 1906
friction-drive Maurer-Union, a 1917 Daniels, the
Norway-built Bjerring of 1920, the Hanomag, and
the scaled-down 1912 Cadillac which was King
Olav V's first car. In addition, the museum has
about 15 unrestored cars.

Bjerring, 1920. Courtesy Norsk Teknisk Museum,
Oslo, Norway

Benz, 1895 and NSU Ro80. Courtesy Norsk Teknisk
Museum, Oslo, Norway

101

Mercedes-Benz, 1934. Courtesy Museu do Automovel, Caramulo, Portugal

PORTUGAL

Museu do Automovel,
Caramulo,
between Coimbra and Viseu
Open every day June–October 10.00–18.00
November–May every day except Monday
10.00–17.00

Dr de Lacerda's famous collection at Caramulo, the only motor museum in Portugal that is open to the public, contains about 34 cars and twenty motor cycles and bicycles; many are on loan, so may be liable to change. The most interesting exhibits are the rare 1902 two-cyclinder Darracq 12 h.p., a Brescia Bugatti of 1923 and Type 35B Grand Prix car of 1927, two Rolls-Royces of 1911 and 1912, a 1914 Abadal, 1925 Delaugère-Clayette, 1935 500K and 1938 Grosser Mercedes-Benz, 1937 Type 812 supercharged Cord, and the 1954 Maserati 250F Grand Prix car.

REPUBLIC OF IRELAND

Blarney Veteran Car Museum,
Blarney Castle,
County Cork
Open every day 10.00–19.00

This collection houses about 20 cars, all well preserved, some of them on loan. They include Sunbeam-Mabley, De Dion Bouton, Arrol-Johnston, Wolseley-Siddeley, Wolseley, Adler, Talbot, Morris and Ford, mostly of the pre-1914 period.

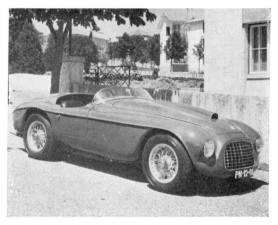

Ferrari, 1950. Courtesy Museu do Automovel, Caramulo, Portugal

Minerva, 1921. Courtesy Museu do Automovel, Caramulo, Portugal

Chenard-Walcker, 1925. Courtesy Museu do Automovel, Caramulo, Portugal

Maserati Formula I Grand Prix car, 1954. Courtesy Museu do Automovel, Caramulo, Portugal

SOVIET UNION

Polytechnical Museum,
Novaya Ploshad 3–4,
Moscow
Open every day except Mondays and last day of month
Tuesday and Thursday 13.00–21.00
Wednesday, Friday, Saturday, Sunday 10.00–18.00
The Polytechnical Museum in Moscow has as its theme the history of science and technology in general, but the automotive gallery contains about 400 items. These include about 40 engines of Russian manufacture, and 50 motor vehicles, some in model form. Of these some are foreign, but the most important are Russian, dating from the pre-First World War period. The oldest Russian car shown is a 1911 Russo-Baltique, but among the 'foreigners' are an 1898 Stoewer from Germany and a 1901 French De Dion Bouton.

Russo-Baltique, 1911. Courtesy Polytechnical Museum, Moscow, Soviet Union

AMO-F-15, 1924 (model). Courtesy Polytechnical Museum, Moscow, Soviet Union

SPAIN

Museo del Ejercito,
C/Mendez, Nunez, No. 1,
Madrid 14
Opening seasons and times not communicated
The Army Museum of Spain, which is open to the public, contains a number of military vehicles of historic interest.

Museo del Automovil de Salvador Claret,
Hostal del Rolls,
Sils,
Gerona
Opening seasons and times not communicated
Only now are motor museums being opened to the public in Spain, which is not surprising, since even though early cars have tended to survive there in large numbers, they have been regarded as everyday transport rather than as museum material. Only now is the modern car so plentiful that the old one is regarded as historic and deserving preservation. The Claret collection was the first to be shown to the public, and includes over 100 cars and motor cycles.

*
Hotel Rosamar,
Lloret del Mar
Opening seasons and times not communicated
This collection is known to exist, but no details were forthcoming at the time of writing. Don Pedro Fontanals has about a dozen cars on show. The museum building is part of the hotel.

SWEDEN

Frederiksdal Open-Air Museum,
Halsingborg Museum,
near Halsingborg
Open every day April–October 10.00–16.00 or 19.00 according to season
The Frederiksdal Open-Air Museum, which is a branch of the Halsingborg Museum, has four cars on show in the carriage hall. They include one of Halsingborg manufacture; the machine made by C. Jonsson in 1898. There is also a 1937 Minerva. The museum itself is generally given over to illustrating Swedish country life in past centuries by means of full-size exhibits such as houses and other buildings.

Tekniska Museet,
Museivagen 7,
N. Djurgarden,
Stockholm No
Open every day
Weekdays 10.00–16.00 Weekends 12.00–16.00
The Stockholm Museum of Science and
Technology has a Machinery Hall that contains
steam engines, locomotives, aero engines and
aircraft, bicycles, and about 10, at any one time,
of the Museum's 40 or so motor vehicles.
Naturally the most notable among the latter are
machines of Swedish manufacture, which include
the original 1897 Vabis, Scanias of 1902 and 1903,
a 1910 Atvidaberg, 1911 Scania-Vabis, 1923 Thulin,
and Helios, Vabis and Tidaholm commercial and
public service vehicles. Americans include an
1908 International Auto Buggy, Milburn and
Detroit electrics, and 1920 Locomobile. There is
an 1896 Léon Bollée, 1909 Motobloc, 1906
Phänomobil, and 1931 Bentley. The motor cycles
number about 20.

Svedinos Bil-och Flygmuseum,
Ugglarp,
between Halmstad and Falkenberg
Open July–15 August 9.00–21.00
15 August–15 September 9.00–19.00
This is Sweden's largest motor museum, with
some 80 vehicles. They take in Jöns Olsson's 1898
Büllerbilen, a 1920 Thulin and Volvos of 1928 and
1929 and a 1908 Tidaholm (all from Sweden); from
Germany and Austria the 1908 Piccolo, a 1911
Gräf und Stift rescued from the seabed, a rare
aerodynamic Adler of 1938, and examples of 1937
Horch, 1912 Phänomobil and 1912 Puch; while
from France is a Renault dated 1903.
Czechoslovakia is represented by Tatras of 1938
and 1951. Since Sweden was a ready market for
American cars, the latter are well represented by
Haynes (1918), Seneca (1920), and Anderson
(1923), as well as by more commonly-seen breeds.
These include a 1918 Pierce-Arrow and a 1936
Cord. Only the earliest Volvos in the collection
can be mentioned here; it houses others, of the
1930s. There are also aircraft.

Berthold Ericsson, 1935. Courtesy Tekniska Museet, Stockholm, Sweden

Volvo, 1928. Courtesy Svedinos Bilmuseum, Ugglarp, Sweden

Volvo, 1935. Courtesy Vatterbygdens Automobilmuseum, Huskvarna, Sweden

Vatterbygdens Automobil Museum,
Motell Vatterleden, E 4,
Huskvarna – Granna
Open every day July 10.00–20.00
Sundays only mid-May to mid-September 12.00–18.00
This museum has about 16 restored cars on show,
and others in course of restoration. The former
include Fords of 1911, 1913, and 1926, examples of
Apperson, Chevrolet, Buick, Whippet, Nash and
Chrysler, a 1938 Horch, two Opels of the 1930s, a
1950 Moskvitch, two Volvo buses of 1935 and 1937,
and a 1927 Tidaholm fire truck. There are seven
motor cycles on display, and three Volvo buses of
1935–8.

Landskrona Museum,
Adolf Fredriks Kasern,
Landskrona
Open every day 13.00–17.00
This is a local museum, in the sense that it
features local products, among them the products
of the Thulin concern, to which two rooms are
devoted. The Thulin exhibits include motor
vehicles and aeroplanes. The former embrace a
motor sleigh, an ambulance, and a passenger car;
but most of the items on show are connected
with aviation: engines, propellers, and a 1918 Type
NA aeroplane.

* *

Industrihistoriska Samling Arna,
Gothenburg
Opening seasons and times not communicated
There are said to be about 15 cars in this museum:
no further data has been provided.

* *

Gamla Bilsalongen,
Svanfors,
between Skelleftea and Boliden
Open every day mid-June to mid-August
Weekdays 10.00–12.00, 14.00–18.00
Sundays 14.00–18.00 Rest of year Sundays only
14.00–18.00
This small collection, totalling about 20 cars, has
an international flavour – examples are the 1903
Regal, 1908 Wolseley, 1912 Minerva and Opel, and
1913 Panhard-Levassor.

Skokloster's Motor Museum,
Skokloster,
via Sigtuna
Open every day summer months 11.00–17.00
winter months 11.00–16.00
The cars at the holiday centre at Skokloster, which
number about 30, include a Renault dated 1899,
1910 Motobloc, 1920 Citroen, and 1931 Delage
from France; an Austin of 1911 from Britain; a
1923 Horch; an Austro-Daimler of the same
decade; and King Gustav's 1939 Cadillac. Part of
the exhibition is reserved for Swedish vehicles,
which embrace a 1912 Scania-Vabis, some Volvos,
and a Tidaholm fire truck. Perhaps even more
interesting than the cars are the motor cycles:
1896 Hildebrand und Wolfmuller, 1908 La
Parisienne, 1909 FN, and some Swedish machines.

A general view of Skokloster's Motor Museum.
Courtesy Skokloster's Motor Museum, Skokloster,
Sweden

Ystads Museer,
Ystad
Open every day
The Ystad museum on the south coast of Sweden
has one really notable exhibit: the Cederholm
steamer of 1894.

Cederholm, 1894. Courtesy Ystads Museer, Ystad, Sweden

SWITZERLAND

Musée de l'Automobile,
Chateau de Grandson,
Lake Neuchatel,
Vaud

Open every day 9.00–18.00

This important collection has between thirty and forty motor vehicles, of which the most significant (though less numerous) are of Swiss origin. These comprise the 1895 Egg, 1901 Dumont and 1909 Turicum. However, Switzerland has always imported most of its cars, a state of affairs reflected in the fact that the rest of the exhibits are foreign. They include an 1895 Peugeot (the earliest), 1897 Rochet, 1900 Larroumet et Lagarde, the highly unusual 1904 Cameron, a racing Type 23 Bugatti and Amilcar G6 of 1924 and 1926 respectively, a Type 35 Grand Prix Bugatti of the latter year, a miniature Type 52 electric car of the same make, and a variety of post-Second World War competition machines. The rarest of these is probably the scaled-down 1948 Cisitalia, like the Type 52 Bugatti built for children.

Popp, 1898. Courtesy Swiss Transport Museum, Lucerne, Switzerland

Berna, 1902. Courtesy Swiss Transport Museum, Lucerne, Switzerland

Swiss Transport Museum,
Lidostrasse 5,
6000 Lucerne
*Open every day mid-March–mid-November
9.00–18.00 mid-November–mid-March Sunday
10.00–18.00, afternoons only Tuesday, Thursday,
Saturday*
The Swiss Transport Museum aims at embracing
the history and contemporary development of all
forms of land, water and air transport and
communications. They are illustrated in
photographs, graphic designs, models, engines
and vehicles. There is a library, and the two
restaurants are to be found in Switzerland's oldest
lake steamer, dating from 1847, and the oldest
dining car in the country. Naturally, the emphasis
is on Swiss transport and communications, and
the most interesting part of the 30-strong
motor-vehicle display is that devoted to native
products. Among them are the 1898 Popp. 1902
Berna, 1907 Turicum, 1905 eight-cylinder Dufaux
racing car, 1908 Ajax, 1919 Piccard-Pictet, and
Orion, Saurer, Fischer and Martini chassis. The
foreign vehicles in the collection are multi-
national, with Clément-Bayard, Panhard-Levassor,
Renault and Hispano-Suiza from France,
Oldsmobile, Ford, and Willys-Overland from
America, Adler and Mercedes-Benz (a 1934 Type
W25 Grand Prix car, this) from Germany, Lancia
from Italy, and Rolls-Royce from Britain – as is
appropriate for a country that has always
imported most of its cars.

Feuerwehrmuseum Basel,
Kornhausgasse 18,
Basle
Opening seasons and times not communicated
Basle's fire service museum includes a steam
pumper of 1905.

Zweirad-Museum,
Garage Edy Bühler,
8633 Wolfhausen,
Zürich
Opening seasons and times not communicated
This, as the name suggests, is a motor-cycle and
bicycle museum, but nothing more is known
about it.

Fischer, 1913. Courtesy Swiss Transport Museum, Lucerne, Switzerland

Ajax, 1908. Courtesy Swiss Transport Museum, Lucerne, Switzerland

Adler, 1910. Courtesy Swiss Transport Museum, Lucerne, Switzerland

UNITED STATES OF AMERICA
Arkansas

Museum of Automobiles,
Route 3,
Petit Jean Mountain,
Morrilton,
Arkansas
Open every day 10.00–17.00

The Winthrop Rockefeller collection, situated not far from the Rockefeller home, is in a modern building in a beautiful mountain setting. In interest, its 50-odd cars are far above average among those in private collections, for they include two Napiers build for the Gordon Bennett races of 1903 and 1904, a 1908 Grand Prix Mercedes, an extremely early Rolls Royce Silver Ghost of 1907 and three Stutzes, among them a 1932 DV32 and a 1914 Bearcat. One of the very first front-engined Panhard-Levassors, dated 1892, contrasts vividly with the 1910 Cretor's Popcorn Wagon, and with two *autobahn*-cruisers of the 1930s, the Mercedes-Benz 500K and 540K. Around a third of the cars on show are in fact foreign. Attached to the Museum is PJA Pneumatic, a concern that manufactures obsolete tyres for early cars.

California

* * *
The Jack Passey Jr Collection,
3210 South Bascom Avenue, San Jose,
California
Open every day Spring–Fall 14.00–18.00

Mr Jack Passey Jr's collection concentrates upon the impressive products of the 'classic' era. It includes representatives of Cadillac, Duesenberg, Lincoln, Packard, Pierce-Arrow, and Wills Sainte Claire. There are about 50 vehicles in all.

Miller's Horse and Buggy Ranch,
9425 Yosemite Boulevard,
Modesto,
California
Open every day

The ten motor vehicles in this collection include some rarities, such as a Success Auto Buggy of 1906 and a 1910 Detroit electric, and at the other end of the scale, a 1915 Pierce Arrow and a 16-cylinder Cadillac with ambulance body. There is a 1906 Sears-Roebuck, and a 1912 Studebaker. As the name of the collection suggests, it concentrates on horsedrawn vehicles, but there are a number of bicycles as well.

Exterior of the Museum of Automobiles. Courtesy Museum of Automobiles, Morrilton, Arkansas

Rolls Royce, 1907. Courtesy Museum of Automobiles, Morrilton, Arkansas

Lozier, 1912. Courtesy Museum of Automobiles, Morrilton, Arkansas

Briggs Cunningham Automotive Museum,
250 E. Baker Street,
Costa Mesa,
California
Open every day June–September 10.00–17.00
Closed Monday and Tuesday October–May
With cars he built himself, Briggs S. Cunningham carried the flag for the United States in international sports-car racing at Le Mans between 1950 and 1955. Some of the machines he used, including the original 'Le Monstre' of 1950, the Model C-1 of 1951, the 1953 C-4R and C-3, and the 1955 Model C-6R (the last model) are on display. But these are only a few of over 70 cars shown, dating from 1911. They form a notably distinguished collection that embraces a 1927 Bugatti Royale, a 1913 Grand Prix Peugeot, a 1914 Grand Prix Mercedes, 1927 Grand Prix Delage, and 1919 eight-cylinder Indianapolis Ballot; a model SSJ Duesenberg (of which only a handful were built), and the H6C Hispano-Suiza which won against the Stutz in the famous challenge at Indianapolis in 1928. Beside such 'stars' as these, the other exhibits, which would make the name of any other collection, are left in the shade, even though they include 8 Litre and $4\frac{1}{2}$ Litre supercharged Bentleys, Bugatti Type 55, a 1917 Cunningham (no relation to Briggs Cunningham's cars), and no fewer than four racing Ferraris and one 12-cylinder Cistalia among the postwar racing cars; also a V12 Packard, V16 Cadillac and V16 Marmon of the 1930s, a Mercer Raceabout of 1912, a DV32 Super Bearcat Stutz of 1932, and a 1933 MG K3 Magnette. There is even an example of the Type 52 electric Bugatti of 1926, made for rich children. If not sated by splendour on such a scale, the visitor can then turn to the engine and chassis component displays, among which is represented the W-163 Grand Prix Mercedes-Benz of 1938–9.

Cunningham, 1951. Courtesy Briggs Cunningham Automotive Museum, Costa Mesa, California

General view in the Los Angeles County Museum. Courtesy County Museum, Los Angeles, California

Wills Sainte-Claire, 1922. Courtesy Briggs Cunningham Automotive Museum, Costa Mesa, California

Los Angeles County Museum of Natural History,
Exposition Park,
900 Exposition Boulevard,
Los Angeles,
California
*Open every day except Mondays and public holidays
10.00–17.00*
The Los Angeles County Museum has a collection
of over 30 vehicles, an unusually high proportion
being of special interest. These include an
air-cooled Aerocar of 1907, a 1911 American
Underslung, a Black Motor Buggy of 1906, the
experimental Burtnett-Brunell twin of 1920,
another experiment in the form of the 1901
Tuckermobile Motor Buggy, a 1912 Little, 1910
Welch and gasoline-powered White of 1917, the
gasoline-electric Woods Dual Power of the same
year, a 1932 Model J. Duesenberg, and two racing-
cars – an overhead-camshaft Stutz of 1915, and a
1927 Miller front wheel drive machine. A modern

car, but a very fine one, is the BMW Type 507 of
1957 with Loewy-designed body that was the
prototype of that for the Studebaker Avanti. The
commercial vehicle on show, the air-cooled 1903
Knox, was Los Angeles' first delivery truck.
Engines of interest are one from a six-cylinder
Model K Ford of about 1907, and an air-cooled
Franklin six of around 1923–5.

Movieland Cars of the Stars,
Knotts Berry Farm,
Buena Park,
California
Opening seasons and times not communicated
This collection, formerly at Wagon Weel
Junction, Oxnard, California, was being moved to
the above address at the time of writing. Over 100
cars and motor cycles were on display, many of
the cars being associated with Hollywood actors
(such as Al Jolson's 1929 Mercedes) or with films.

Peerless, 1903. Courtesy Veteran Car Museum, Denver, Colorado

Colorado

Veteran Car Museum,
2030 South Cherokee Street,
Denver,
Colorado
Open every day 9.00–17.00 (Sundays in afternoon only)
Mr Arthur G. Rippey's original collection, started in 1945, was dispersed between 1966 and 1968, but he then began to assemble another one, which contains about two dozen cars covering nearly 70 years of history. Among them are a very rare 1903 twin-cylinder Peerless, a 1906 Buick, and a 1916 Detroit electric. It is unusual to see foreign cars such as a 1913 Lagonda and a 1923–4 Delaunay-Belleville, uncommon anywhere, in the United States. The collection's 1929 Pierce-Arrow is accompanied by a 1937 Pierce-Arrow TraveLodge caravan, made when the company's car-manufacturing life had almost come to an end.

Forney Transportation Museum,
Valley Highway and Speer Boulevard,
Fort Collins,
Colorado
Opening seasons and times not communicated
This immense collection, totalling around 200 motor and horsedrawn vehicles, has cars with interesting associations, among them the 1927 Rolls-Royce that belonged to Prince Aly Khan, and the aviatrix Amelia Earhart's 'Gold Bug'. Early Vauxhalls are not often seen in American museums, and here is a 1912 example. There are also an 1899 Locomobile steamer, 1901 Searchmont, 1906 Pope-Tribune, 1912 Nyberg and Renault, 1914 Detroit Electric, and oddities such as the Neracar, and the 1920 six-wheeled Hispano-Suiza with 25-foot wheelbase. The museum takes in bicycles, steam engines, railway rolling stock, aircraft, horsedrawn carriages and historic costumes as well.

Chrysler Imperial, 1933. Courtesy Veteran Car Museum, Denver, Colorado

* * *
Buckskin Joe's Antique Auto Museum,
Canon City,
Colorado
Open every day April 15–October 1 7.30–19.00
There are over 20 cars in this museum. No further details were provided.

Connecticut
Antique Auto Museum,
Slater Street at Interstate 84,
Manchester,
Connecticut
Open every day 10.00–20.00
This new collection shows about 26 cars, almost all fully restored and in working order. They include 1915 Cole and Stellite, 1910 Knox, 1925 Renault, 1916 Metz, 1922 Cadillac, 1924 Lincoln, 1938 Horch, Packards of 1922, 1928 and 1937, 1917 Oakland, and 1939 Bantam.

District of Columbia
Museum of History and Technology,
Smithsonian Institution,
Washington, D.C.
Open every day except at Christmas
April–August: 10.00–21.00
September–March: 10.00–17.30
As far as the earliest self-propelled vehicles of the United States are concerned, the Vehicle Hall in the Museum of History and Technology houses one of the country's most important collections. It includes a steam velocipede made by Sylvester Roper, the first man in America to make practical self-propelled vehicles in any numbers, an 1880 steam tricycle by Long, the first Duryea of 1893 and the first Haynes of 1894, the first air-cooled Franklin sold, of 1902, and three Wintons – the racing Bullets numbers 1 and 2, and the 1903 20 h.p. model driven by Dr Nelson Jackson from coast to coast: the first car to achieve this. The Selden, the subject of the most celebrated patent battle in American automotive history, is represented by a model of the vehicle alleged to have been built in 1879. Some more early machines that are important or otherwise interesting are the 1894 Balzer quadricycle, an Olds brothers product of 1897, a 1902 White steamer and a Simplex speedster of 1912. Being the national museum of transportation, the 40-strong collection covers most other types of

mechanical road vehicle as well: there are Pope and Harley-Davidson motor-cycles of 1913, and a 1918 Cleveland, while among the commercial and public service vehicles are a White bus of 1917, a 1911 Sears light delivery truck, an American La France fire truck of 1920, and a 1930 Mack Model AC Bulldog truck. One of the first Jeeps is there, in the form of a Bantam-built model of 1940. Finally, there are extensive collections of bicycles and horsedrawn vehicles. Not all of the machines mentioned above are necessarily on show: about half the Museum's collection are kept in the reference collection for lack of space in the Vehicle Hall, and are displayed in rotation.

Simplex, 1912. Courtesy Smithsonian Institution, Washington, D.C.

Duryea, 1893: America's first successful gasoline-engined car. Courtesy Smithsonian Institution, Washington, D.C.

Florida

Bellm Cars of Yesterday,
5500 North Tamiami Trail,
Sarasota,
Florida
Open every day Monday – Saturday 8.30 – 18.00
Sunday 9.30 – 18.00

The exhibition known as Bellm Cars and Music of Yesterday houses not only a unique collection of mechanical music-makers, including nickelodeons, phonographs, band organs, hurdy-gurdies, and 500 music boxes, but also some 85 early cars dating from 1897. Among them are a 1901 Oldsmobile, 1902 Stanley steamer, 1906 Pope-Toledo and Cadillac, 1907 Brush, 1911 Staver Special (the only one built), a 1930 Model J Duesenberg, and a Rolls Royce Silver Ghost originally built for the Czarina of Russia and later owned by the circus magnate John Ringling. Particular rarities include the 1902 Murray, 1905 Mier, 1908 PMC, 1909 'Dreadnaughty' and Sterling, 1914 Saginaw cyclecar, 1930 Ruxton and 1916 Dorris.

Museum of Speed,
Highway 1,
South Daytona,
Florida
Open every day January, March, April, May,
September, October, November, December:
9.00 – 18.00
February, June, July, August: 9.00 – 21.00

Daytona Beach has been the scene of many of history's most important attacks on land speed records, so it is fitting that here should be seen Sir Malcolm Campbell's famous Bluebird of 1935, which took the world's land speed record in that year at 276.82 m.p.h., and the remains, less the engine, of the Stanley steamer 'Rocket', which in the hands of Fred Marriott, attained 127.66 m.p.h. in 1906. The engine is in the Smithsonian Institution (*q.v.*). Here, too, is *Miss America V111*, the speedboat in which Gar Wood defeated both Sir Henry Segrave and Kaye Don in *Miss England* and *Miss England 11* respectively. At Daytona are also shown record-breaking motor cycles and dragsters, and the world's fastest kart.

A general view of the exterior, Bellm Cars of Yesterday, Sarasota, Florida.
Courtesy Bellm Cars of Yesterday

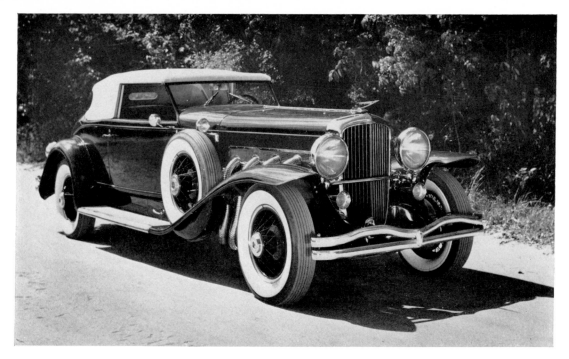

Duesenberg Model SJ, 1934. Courtesy Early American Museum, Silver Springs, Florida

Stutz Super Bearcat, 1932. Courtesy Early American Museum, Silver Springs, Florida

Early American Museum,
Silver Springs,
Florida
Open every day 9.00–21.00
This museum, like so many, sets out to illustrate many sides of early American life, in this case including fashions, dolls, and the circus. There are some 100 cars and carriages shown, which include an 1898 Hertel, 1900 Prescott steamer, 1903 Crestmobile, 1909 Stanley, 1910 Kelsey, one of the revolutionary Rumplers (of 1918), 1914 Pierce Arrow, a 1919 Auto Red Bug cyclecar, 1930 V16 Cadillac, 1931 Invicta, and a 1934 Duesenberg.

Elliott Museum,
Route 1,
Stuart,
Florida
Open every day 13.00–17.00
The Vehicular Wing of the Elliott Museum, run by the Martin County Historical Society, contains about 35 cars in varying states of completeness and roadworthiness, together with bicycles, motor cycles and fire engines. Those that are complete include a 1902 Stanley, 1903 Pierce Motorette, 1907 Maxwell, 1909 Ford Model T, 1909 and 1911 Hupmobile, a rare 1910 Empire speedster, an Orient Buckboard and (in total contrast) a 1913 Detroit electric Opera Coupé, and 1903 Reo. There is heavy metal in the shape of a 1915 V8 Cadillac, Twin Six Packard, 1909 Thomas Flyer, 1923 Pierce-Arrow, 1913 Simplex, and 1924 Rolls-Royce Silver Ghost. Among the oddities is the chassis of a three-wheeled Kelsey.

Georgia
* * *
Stone Mountain Antique Auto Museum,
2045 Robson Place N.E.,
Atlanta,
Georgia
Open every day 10.00–17.00
10.00–18.00 in summer
Mr C. T. Protsman's museum has about 30 cars, which display a catholic taste: under the same roof can be seen some of the most distinguished classics, such as a Stutz DV 32 and a Lincoln dual cowl phaeton of 1928; and also a curved-dash Oldsmobile of a generation before, in Pie Wagon guise. Other cars on show include an 1899 Stanley steamer and 1913 Car-Nation.

Illinois
Museum of Science and Industry,
57th Street and South Lake Shore Drive,
Jackson Park,
Chicago,
Illinois
Open every day except at Christmas
Winter months Monday–Saturday 9.30–16.00
Summer months 9.30–17.30
Sundays and holidays 10.00–18.00
The Museum of Science and Industry is housed in what was the Fine Arts building erected for the 1893 World's Columbian Exposition at Chicago, since restored. Its motor vehicles, which are important if not very numerous (about 30), include a Bernardi (more properly Miari & Giusti) of the 1890s, 1896 Benz, 1902 McIntyre, 1903 Stevens-Duryea, 1907 Stoddard-Dayton, 1909 Gleason, 1910 National raceabout, 1911 Marmon racing car, 1911 Simplex, 1913 Metz and Mercedes, 1914 Brewster and Marmon, a 1920 Alfa Romeo, and a 1929 Model J Duesenberg at one end of the time scale, and Craig Breedlove's jet-powered 'Spirit of America', the first land vehicle to exceed 500 m.p.h., at the other. Even more outlandish is the 'Chizler', the first dragster to exceed 200 m.p.h. at the end of a standing quarter-mile; a record set up in 1960.

Fagan's Antique and Classic Automobile Museum,
162nd and Claremont Avenue,
Markham,
Illinois
Open every day 8.00–21.00
Fords are a speciality of Mr Fagan's collection; among them are a 1903 Model A, a 1906 Model K, and a 1908 Model S. He also shows a 1908 Holsman, a 1932 Stutz, and displays of horsedrawn vehicles and exhibits illustrative of local rural life.

Indiana
Henry H. Blommel Historical Auto Collection,
Route 5,
Connersville,
Indiana
Opening seasons and times not communicated
Mr Henry Blommel's collection specializes in Indiana firms: McFarlan, Lexington, Empire, Auburn, and Cord.

Brush, 1904. Courtesy Chicago Museum of Science and Industry, Chicago, Illinois

Bernardi, ca. 1896. Courtesy Chicago Museum of Science and Industry, Chicago, Illinois

Milburn, 1925. Courtesy Chicago Museum of Science and Industry, Chicago, Illinois

Brewster, 1914–5. Courtesy Chicago Museum of Science and Industry, Chicago, Illinois

Goodwin Museum,
200 South Main Street,
Frankfort,
Indiana
Opening seasons and times not communicated
Mr William Goodwin's dozen or so cars include
some unusual items, such as a 1901 Frisbie and a
1904 Gatts, and what is claimed to be the biggest
motor hearse in existence, of make unspecified.
There are also a 1904 Haynes-Apperson, 1914
Stutz Bearcat and 1918 Stutz Bulldog, 1915
Briscoe, a 1927 Bugatti Grand Prix car, a Cord 812
of 1937, a 1936 Auburn, and Duesenbergs Model
J of 1930 and 1932. There are many bicycles.

Elwood Haynes Museum,
1915 South Webster Street,
Kokomo,
Indiana
Open every day except Monday
Tuesday–Saturday 13.00–16.00
Sunday 13.00–17.00
This is the house which Elwood Haynes himself
occupied until his death in 1925. The
automobile exhibits comprise examples of Haynes
of 1905 and 1924, and an Apperson Jackrabbit.

Indianapolis Motor Speedway Museum,
4790 West 16th Street,
Indianapolis,
Indiana
Open every day 9.00–17.00
This unique collection of racing cars, opened in
1956, is devoted to machines that have performed
on the famous 'brickyard' circuit (since asphalted),
which was opened in 1909. The first 500-mile
classic race was held here in 1911, and the winner
on that occasion, Ray Harroun's Marmon, is among
the exhibits today. Others among the 12 winners
shown are the National of 1912, René Thomas's
Delage (1913), Jimmy Murphy's Duesenberg
(1922), Louis Meyer's 1928 Miller, Wilbur Shaw's
Maserati which won in 1939 and 1940, the Thorne
Special (1946), the Lou Moore Blue Crown front-
wheel-drive car driven to victory by Mauri Rose in
1947 and 1948, and the 1964 Sheraton-Thompson
Special. Further cars present are a 1901 Panhard-
Levassor, a 1903 Premier built for the first
Vanderbilt Cup race, Tetzlaff's 1912
Indianapolis Fiat, Eddie Rickenbacker's
Duesenberg of 1914, the Cummins Diesel Special
that set up new lap records in 1952, and a 1954
Grand Prix Mercedes-Benz.

A general view of the Museum. Courtesy Indianapolis Motor Speedway Museum, Indianapolis, Indiana

Maserati, 1939. Courtesy Indianapolis Motor Speedway Museum, Indianapolis, Indiana

Delage, 1913. Courtesy Indianapolis Motor Speedway Museum, Indianapolis, Indiana

Duesenberg, 1921. Courtesy Indianapolis Motor Speedway Museum, Indianapolis, Indiana

Early Wheels Museum,
817 Wabash Avenue,
Terre Haute,
Indiana
*Open Monday–Friday except public holidays
10.00–16.00*
The Early Wheels Museum embraces around 30 cars from 1897 to 1927, horsedrawn wagons, bicycles, and locomotives. These vehicles are owned by the Indianapolis Motor Speedway, and they may be incorporated in the Museum there (*q.v.*) so visitors should make a particularly careful check before calling.

Iowa

*

The Schaffer Museum,
Spirit Lake,
Iowa
Opening seasons and times not communicated
This collection was known to exist in 1969, but no details are forthcoming at the time of writing.

Kansas

* * *

Abilene Auto Museum,
Abilene Center,
Abilene,
Kansas
Open weekends only 11.00–17.00
That part of Mr L. L. Lacer's collection that is on public view consists of about 20 cars. They take in such machines as a 1929 Brooklands Riley, 1932 Cadillac, and 1939 Delahaye.

Great Smith, 1908. Courtesy Kansas State Historical Society Museum, Topeka, Kansas

Kansas State Historical Museum,
Memorial Building,
10th and Jackson,
Topeka,
Kansas
*Open every day except public holidays
Monday–Friday 8.15–17.00 Saturday 8.15–16.00
Sunday 13.00–16.30*
The museum of the Kansas State Historical Society, as its name suggests, covers the whole history of the state. The Smith car and its successor the Great Smith, built in Topeka between 1902 and 1908, were a very small part of that history, but the museum has a 1908 example, and also a Thomas Flyer of about the same period.

Maine

Boothbay Railway Museum,
Route 27,
Boothbay,
Maine
*Open mid-May–early October
Open week-ends only Memorial Day–June 16
Open every day June 17–Labor Day 10.00–17.00*
As its name suggests, this is a museum that is devoted mainly to the railway age, but there is also a display of about 25 early cars, mostly on loan.

Massachusetts

Heritage Plantation of Sandwich,
Grove and Pine Streets,
Sandwich,
Massachusetts
Open every day June–October 10.00–17.00
The Heritage Plantation is one of many museums of American history, in this case concentrating upon guns and model soldiers. The motor car collection is large, but only about 35 can be shown at any one time in the Round Barn. The museum's property includes an early Stevens-Duryea, Waltham and Sears highwheelers, an Oldsmobile racing car, a Mercer, a Stutz Bearcat, an Auburn, two Cadillacs (one with 16 cylinders), a Model J Duesenberg, three Packards, and examples of Cord, Franklin, Kissel, LaSalle, Lincoln, and Springfield-built Rolls Royce.

Museum of Motoring Progress,
Larz Anderson Park,
15 Newton Street,
Brookline,
Massachusetts
Open every day except Monday 13.00–17.00
The Museum at Larz Anderson Park, not far from
the centre of Boston, is in what was a coach-
house modelled on the château of Chaumont in
France. The exhibits consist of the cars of the
Larz Anderson collection together with vehicles
lent by members of the Veteran Car Club of
America, and some donations. The museum is an
educational, non-profit-making organization,
including not only cars but also motor-cycles,
bicycles, horsedrawn vehicles, literature,
photographs and drawings. Among the most
interesting of the 80-odd motor vehicles are a
Dudgeon steamer of 1867, a 1900 Rochet-Schneider,
a Winton of 1901 (said to have a racing history),
a 1903 Gardner-Serpollet steamer, a large Fiat
roadster of 1907, an elegant 1908 Bailey electric,
an Ohio electric of 1917, a front-wheel-drive
Christie fire tractor, and a V12 Packard that was
used by President Franklin D. Roosevelt.

* * *

Sturbridge Auto Museum,
Old Sturbridge Village,
Route 20,
Sturbridge,
Massachusetts
Open every day June–August 10.30–21.30
Weekends April, May, November 12.30–17.30
Weekends September–October 10.30–17.30
Mr Harold J. Kenneway's collection of about two
dozen cars takes in vehicles of every type –
gasoline, steam and electric – and of every period
from 1897 to 1939.

* * *

Edaville Railroad Museum,
South Carver,
Massachusetts
Open every day June 15–Labor Day
Weekdays 10.00–17.00 Sunday 12.00–17.00
Also some weekends in Spring and Fall
The Edaville Railroad Museum, as well as early
rail relics, also has motor cars, fire engines, a
rifle collection, and a reconstructed 19th-century
village, besides the railway itself. It is associated
with Steamtown USA in Vermont (*q.v*).

Michigan

Henry Ford Museum and Greenfield Village,
Dearborn,
Michigan
*Open every day except Thanksgiving, Christmas,
New Year's Day 9.00–17.00 June 15–Labor Day
9.00–18.30*
The Henry Ford Museum and the associated
Greenfield Village together form one of the most
extensive and important collections of early
Americana in the United States. The
transportation collection is only one among many,
embracing the history of the country from the
1620s to the recent past (houses, shops, factories
and laboratories, and many of the decorative and
mechanical arts); and in the transportation
collection, motor cars have to share space with
commercial vehicles and aircraft. It is possible to
mention only some of the most outstanding of the
200-odd cars shown: Sylvester Roper's steam
carriage of 1863, contrasting with that most
sophisticated of steam cars, the Doble of 1923;
the 1888 Benz, Henry Ford's '999' racing car of
1902 and his first car, the 1896 quadricycle; the
Selden built in 1907 but alleged to be a replica of
a machine built 30 years before; a Joswin from
the stables of the Kaiser Wilhelm II; a Bugatti
Royale; and the Packard 'Old Pacific' that crossed
the continent in 1903. Otherwise ordinary cars
famous for their associations include Charles
Lindbergh's Franklin, J. Pierpoint Morgan's
Rolls-Royce Silver Ghost, President Taft's 1912
Baker electric, Henry Ford's own Model A, and
Walter Chrysler's Imperial.

Sloan Panorama of Transportation,
303 Walnut Street,
Flint,
Michigan
Open every day
The Sloan Panorama, part of Flint's College and
Cultural Center, has 43 cars, some of them on
loan, about a dozen horsedrawn vehicles, and
miscellaneous engine, transmission and accessory
exhibits. The Panorama is particularly proud of its
collection of locally-built Chevrolets and Buicks.
These include a Classic Six Chevrolet, a Buick
Model C of 1905, and a Buick 'Bug' racing car of
1910. William C. Durant's first vehicle, a
horsedrawn Flint Road Cart, is also represented.

Woodland Cars of Yesteryear,
6504 28th Street S.E.,
Grand Rapids,
Michigan
Open every day except Christmas and
Thanksgiving 10.00–20.00
The 25 or so exhibits in this museum change
frequently, as the owner points out, but it includes
some vehicles unlikely to be seen in many other
places in the United States, such as a 1925
Minerva from Belgium. Indeed, the Krastin
electric, attributed to 1898, is the only one of its
kind. There have also been 1906 Cadillac, Brush,
1908 Buick and International, 1920 Milburn
electric, 1909 air-cooled Richmond, Dodge,
Packard, Oldsmobile, Ford and Chevrolet on show.

Baumgarten Auto Museum,
1181 Lewis Street,
Jackson,
Michigan
Open every day May–October
There are over 60 cars in this museum, most of
them pre-1915, and specializing in locally-built
vehicles. These include a 1910 Cutting, 1909
Jackson, and 1909 Cartercar. There are Buicks of
1906, 1907 and 1909, Renaults of 1905, 1908 and
1912, Franklins of 1905 and 1909, a 1915 Autocar,
1923 Morgan, 1911 Simplex and Koehler, 1903
Pierce Motorette, 1919 Hupmobile, and two
Cadillacs: one of 1907, and a 1932 V12. The trucks
embrace Packard, Diamond T and others.

Gilmore Car Museum,
Hickory Corners,
Michigan
Open Sunday afternoons only, mid-June to
mid-September
Mr Donald S. Gilmore's private collection, on show
here, consists of about 70 cars, including
Bugatti, Cadillac, Daimler, Darracq, Duesenberg,
Franklin, Lincoln, Lozier, Marion Bobcat,
Mercedes, Packard, Pierce-Arrow, Renault, Rolls
Royce, Stevens-Duryea, Stutz, Stanley (several of
these steamers), and White steamer. Another
steamer is the Foster; indeed, steam is Mr
Gilmore's special interest, reflected not only in the
cars mentioned but also in his steam-powered
Falcon, his Foden steam truck, a steam riverboat,
and a narrow-gauge locomotive.

Packard, 1908. Courtesy Gilmore Car Museum, Hickory Corners, Michigan

Bugatti Type 54, 1931. Courtesy Gilmore Car Museum, Hickory Corners, Michigan

Stanley, 1908. Courtesy Gilmore Car Museum, Hickory Corners, Michigan

Cadillac VI6, 1937. Courtesy Gilmore Car Museum, Hickory Corners, Michigan

Holsman, 1909. Courtesy Gilmore Car Museum, Hickory Corners, Michigan

Detroit Historical Museum,
Woodward at Kirby,
Detroit,
Michigan
Open every day except Monday, Christmas and New Year's Day 9.00–18.00
The Detroit Historical Museum, as befits a collection in the home of the American automobile, embraces some unique machines as well as the commoner breed; in all, about two dozen cars and five fire engines, together with wagons, carriages, and other horsedrawn vehicles. Not all are on show at any one time: for lack of space, the exhibits rotate, some always being in store. There is a replica of the 1896 King, Detroit's first car; the one and only Scripps-Booth Bi-Auto-Go, a two-wheeler working on the gyro principle; three Scripps-Booth cyclecars, one a Da Vinci Pup model of 1927-30; no fewer than two Stout Scarabs (half the total built) of 1935 and 1946; a 1935 Indianapolis Miller-Ford with reversed V8 engine providing front wheel drive, and a body from a 1913 Hupmobile, on which was found the first all-steel coachwork to be mass-produced. Three otherwise ordinary machines have special associations: Henry Leland's 1905 Cadillac, with unusual closed body, and two Dodges of 1919, which belonged to the Dodge brothers.

Poll Museum,
Highway 31 and New Holland Street,
Holland,
Michigan
Open every day except Sunday May–September 8.00–18.00
The Poll Museum has around two dozen motor cars, including President Taft's White steamer, a 1903 Oldsmobile, a Rolls-Royce and a Tucker; also fire trucks, bicycles, horsedrawn carriages, and model ships and engines.

Minnesota
* * *
Hemp Old Vehicle Museum,
Country Club Road,
Rochester,
Minnesota
Open every day March–November
Mr Paul L. Hemp's 40 vehicles concentrate upon horsedrawn carriages, steam engines and tractors, but there is also a Model F Ford of 1905.

Missouri
* * *
Kelsey's Antique Cars,
Highway 54,
Camdenton,
Missouri
Open every day April–November
The 40 or so cars in Mr Paul Kelsey's collection include 1899 Mobile and 1906 Stanley steamers, a Velie of 1909, and a 1916 Luverne.

Nebraska
Hastings Museum,
Highway 281 and 14th Street,
Hastings,
Nebraska
Open every day September–May
Monday–Saturday 8.00–17.00
June–August, 8.00–20.00 Sunday 13.00–17.00
The half-dozen cars in this small collection, part of a general museum, comprise a 1903 Cadillac, 1905 Buick, 1907 Reo, 1909 Sears Motor Buggy, 1910 Brush, and 1914 Model T Ford.

Sawyer's Sandhills Museum,
Highway 20,
Valentine,
Nebraska
Open every day from Memorial Day to Labor Day 8.00–20.00
Apart from miscellaneous early Americana, including farm machinery, this museum houses upwards of 20 motor vehicles in running order. Among them are a 1900 steamer, a Schacht twin-cylinder of 1903, a 1908 Brush single-cylinder, a Firestone Columbus of the same year, a 1911 Austro-Daimler, 1913 Imperial, 1916 Patterson, 1917 Grant, an American La France fire truck, and an air-cooled Franklin of 1930.

Harold Warp Pioneer Village,
Highways 6 and 34,
Minden,
Nebraska
Open every day 8.00–dusk
The Harold Warp Pioneer Village exists to show the development of the American frontier scene from around 1830, when mechanization began. The Antique Auto Building houses about 100 cars and trucks; there is also a Fire House in which can be seen appliances from the hand cart to the modern fire truck. The Power House displays early agricultural and industrial machinery.

Nevada

Harrah's Automobile Collection,
Reno,
Nevada

Open every day 10.00–17.00

Mr William Harrah's huge collection, which deserves the epithet fantastic, and aims to illustrate the full history of the motor car, is claimed to be the world's largest – it is certainly the biggest assembly of motor vehicles open to the public at the time of writing. There are well over 1300 cars in it, taking in every possible class and period, from a Riker electric of 1896 to Ferraris of the 1950s. The total number is partly accounted for by including, in a number of instances, as many types and models as possible of a particular make, or, in the case of Ford and Packard, one from every manufacturing year. For example, Mr Harrah has more than 100 Fords from 1903 to 1951, and over 50 examples of Packard and of Franklin. Like the Henry Ford Museum (*q.v.*) another feature is cars owned by famous or distinguished personalities, or with a famous history. In the last category is the Thomas Flyer that won the New York–Paris round-the-world race of 1908. In the space available here, it is almost impossible to give a fair impression of what is shown by naming cars; it must suffice to generalize, and to pick out a few – such as the (very early) 1899 Winton, the twin-cylinder 1904 air-cooled Knox, 1906 Compound (gasoline-powered, but with the piston in the third of its three cylinders actuated by the exhaust gas from the other two), 1908 six-cylinder Stearns, o.h.c. Welch of 1909, the oldest known Mercer (1910) and a Type 35 Raceabout, 1916 Crane-Simplex, 1917 McFarlan, 1921 Heine-Velox (extremely rare), a Stutz Black Hawk speedster of 1927, 1928 Cunningham, 1928 front-wheel-drive Ruxton, 1934 Brewster, a 6CM Maserati racing car of 1936, and a number of Bugattis, Bentleys, Mercedes-Benz and Duesenbergs. Among the cars at the other end of the scale in price and size, if not rarity, we have the Imp and Briggs and Stratton cyclecars, and the American Austin. At any one time, a great many acquisitions are being restored in the workshops attached to the museum, which can also be inspected by visitors. Apart from cars, motor cycles, boats, aircraft and a locomotive are to be seen.

Bugatti Royale, 1931. Courtesy Harrah's Automobile Collection, Reno, Nevada

New Hampshire

* * *

Meredith Auto Museum,
Route 3,
New Hampshire
Open every day June 15 – Labor Day 10.00 – 18.00
The Meredith Auto Museum of about 60 cars includes examples of Stanley steamer, Pathfinder, Stutz, U.S. Long Distance, Rambler, Orient Buckboard and Baker electric, from every period from 1899 to the 1930s. Also to be seen are bicycles, licence plates, parts, and nickelodeons.

New York

Long Island Automotive Museum,
Museum Square,
Southampton,
New York
Open June – September every day, weekends only late May and October
Mr Henry Austin Clark Jr.'s collection is one of the oldest independent automobile museums in the world, having been opened in 1948. It consists of over 150 vehicles, most of them in running order. Among its most important features are its sporting cars (including a 1903 Peerless, 1911 Mercer Raceabout, 1912 Moon, 1911 Simplex, 1919 Stutz Bearcat, 1916 Pierce-Arrow, and 1926 GP Bugatti), and its public service vehicles. The latter embrace a number of fire engines, and several New York buses of different eras, such as a 1925 Fifth Avenue Coach Line machine, a 1931 Yellow Coach and a 1937–8 Queen Mary-type from the same stable which would not look out of place today. The most unusual vehicle in the collection is the one and only 1906 Pungs-Finch Limited; a very large and sporting machine with an overhead camshaft engine.

Upstate Auto Museum,
Route 20,
Bridgewater,
New York
Open every day June – September: 9.00 – 18.00
May and October Sundays only 9.00 – 18.00
This museum, founded 20 years ago and one of the oldest survivors, contains over 100 gasoline, steam and electric cars, and some 50 bicycles. They have not been restored to 'as-new' condition, but are kept in their original state.

North Carolina

Frontier Village,
Highway 321,
Blowing Rock,
North Carolina
Open every day May – October 9.00 – 18.00
This museum of early Americana, in which steam power is the main feature, has around 20 cars and trucks. The latter include a 1918 Nash fire engine and a 1919 Kissel truck.

Ohio

Allen County Museum,
620 West Market Street,
Lima,
Ohio
Open every day except Monday 13.30 – 17.00
The Allen County Historical Society's museum is devoted mainly to preserving relics of the county's past in general, but it contains a 1923 Milburn electric car, a formidable Locomobile sport roadster of 1909, a 1941 Packard, a 1938 La Salle hearse, a 1929 Ahrens-Fox fire engine, and a 1903 Indian motor cycle. Not to be seen in the museum through lack of space, but belonging to the Society, are a Liberty truck of the First World War, and some more modern cars of less interest.

Frederick C. Crawford Auto-Aviation Museum,
10825 East Boulevard,
University Circle,
Cleveland,
Ohio
Open every day except Monday
Tuesday – Saturday 10.00 – 17.00
Sunday 13.00 – 18.00
The Western Reserve Historical Society's vehicle collection, formerly the Thompson Auto Album and Aviation Museum and now the Frederick C. Crawford Auto-Aviation Museum, forms part of the Society's fine Historical Museum devoted to that part of north-eastern Ohio originally known as the Western Reserve of Connecticut. There are over 130 cars in the collection, the bias being towards Cleveland-built machines (Baker, American Gas, Peerless, Winton, White, Templar, Royal Tourist). Others include a (Chicago-built)

Tri-Moto of 1895, a Panhard-Levassor of about 1895 with a curious closed coupé body, a 1903 Elmore, a 1908 Anderson Stanhope, a Duryea phaeton of 1910 with which the collection began in 1937, and classics of the 1920s and 1930s such as Isotta-Fraschini and Marmon V16. A 1936 oddity is a Ford with a stainless steel body; one of half a dozen built. The Baker electric is represented by 1899 and 1900 models; there are several Peerlesses, including the last made (1932), and White steamers of 1902 and 1905. There are fire trucks, including a 1913 White and a 1925 Seagrave; also bicycles, horsedrawn vehicles, and aircraft. These include three Curtiss machines: a 1911 'pusher' seaplane, a 1917 flying boat and a 1920 Oriole.

The museum's restoration shop may be visited, as may the reconstructed 1900s street scene.

* * *
Rodway Classic Era Cars,
1112 Rutherford Road,
Cleveland Heights,
Ohio
Opening seasons and times not communicated
This collection has as its object the accumulation of sport models of the classic era, defined here as the period 1923–32. The result is a fine

assembly of elegant machinery, totalling some 80 cars. The rarities include a Brewster phaeton of 1935, Ford V8-powered; a 1932 Imperia boat-tailed speedster from Belgium; a McFarlan Gentleman's Roadster of 1926; a 1930 Ruxton (front wheel drive) Roadster Runabout; a Viking Convertible Coupé; a Wills Sainte Claire Gray Goose Roadster of 1922; and a 1929 Windsor White Prince Roadster. Better known but no less to be admired are examples of 1929 Auburn, $4\frac{1}{2}$ Litre Bentley, Type 44 Bugatti, dual cowl phaetons from Cadillac, Franklin, Lincoln, and Pierce-Arrow, Chrysler Imperial Roadster, Cord Convertible Coupé, Duesenberg J Convertible Sedan, DuPont Sport Phaeton, Hispano-Suiza H6B, Isotta-Fraschini, Jordan Playboy Roadster, Kissel Gold Bug Speedster, Locomobile Sportif Phaeton, Marmon Roadster, Mercedes-Benz Type K, Mercer Raceabout, Packard Boat Tail Speedster, Peerless Boat Tail Coupé, Rolls-Royce Boat Tail Speedster by Barker and Playboy Roadster by the American coachbuilder Brewster, Studebaker President Roadster, Stutz Black Hawk Speedster and SV16 Bearcat Speedster, and Templar Sportette Touring. The names are a catalogue of the evocative names given to some of the most elegant body styles ever devised.

Locomobile, 1909. Courtesy Allen County Museum, Lima, Ohio

Pennsylvania

Gene Zimmermann's Automobilorama,
Holiday West,
Route 15,
Harrisburg,
Pennsylvania
Open every day 9.00–22.00
Mr Gene Zimmermann's collection of over 250
cars, buses, trucks and fire engines, to which
should be added motor cycles, engines, bicycles
and nickelodeons, is situated in the Holiday Motor
Hotels complex at Harrisburg. The cars take in
Ford models from 1903 to 1932, including a 1907
Model K; Chevrolets from between 1914 and 1939;
Cadillacs of 1903–57 such as a V12 of 1931;
Buicks from 1906 to 1933; Chryslers, Packards,
Pierce Arrows and many others. These latter
include a 1909 Thomas Flyer and a 1922 Kissel
Gold Bug speedster.

Zimmermann, 1909. Courtesy Gene Zimmermann's
Automobilorama, Harrisburg, Pennsylvania

Swigart Museum,
Museum Park,
Route 22,
Huntingdon,
Pennsylvania
Open every day, June – August 10.00–20.00
Weekends May, September, October
This large collection of approximately 200 vehicles
(about a third of them on show) is representative
of every side of American automotive history.
There are gasoline, steam and electric cars,
including a 1906 Studebaker electric built for the
U.S. Senate subway, 1910 Locomobile and
Packard, a 1916 Scripps-Booth, a 1920 Carroll,
1930 Duesenberg, 1931 Marmon, and a Brewster.
Licence plates and name plates to the number of
some 35,000 are also given feature treatment.

Boyertown Museum of Historic Vehicles,
Warwick & Laurel Streets,
Boyertown,
Pennsylvania
Open weekdays 8.00–17.00
The two dozen cars in this museum – which are
in a minority compared with its magnificent
collection of horsedrawn vehicles – are devoted
to vehicles (or bodywork) built in Berks County,
Pennsylvania, among which are some great
rarities. They include a 1902 Duryea, 1905 Boss
steamer, 1912 SGV, 1914 Dile, 1919 Daniels, 1924
Walker electric truck, and a 1928 Cadillac. There
are also motor cycles, bicycles, and fire
appliances.

South Carolina

Joe Weatherly Stock Car Museum,
Darlington Raceway,
Darlington,
South Carolina
*Open every day except winter Saturdays
9.00–12.00, 14.00–17.00*
This museum, which adjoins the Darlington
Raceway for stock cars, contains about ten
famous machines, including the 1950 Plymouth
that won the inaugural Southern 500, the 1963
Ford driven by Glenn Roberts, and Joe
Weatherly's 1964 Mercury. There is an exhibition
of trophies and relics.

South Dakota

* * *

Pioneer Auto Museum,
Highway 16 and 83,
Murdo,
South Dakota
Open every day April–November 7.00–18.00
There are about 90 cars on view in this collection,
some of them rarities such as the 1902 Jewel and
Schacht, the 1904 Fuller, the Spacke cyclecar,
1913 RCH, 1909 Auburn (a very early example of
the make), a 1913 Argo Electric, 1919 Patterson,
and 1928 Cunningham (one of the last made). Also
to be seen are horse-drawn carriages, musical
instruments, toys, and farm equipment including
tractors from between 1917 and 1924.

* * *

Horseless Carriage Museum,
Mount Rushmore Road,
Rapid City,
South Dakota
Open every day April–November 7.00–19.00
This is a small collection, but well worth a visit
for its unusual cars, which include an impressive
Velie speedster of 1910, a 1905 Stanley steamer,
and a 1918 V8 Chevrolet. Other collections of
early Americana cover costumes, guns, toys,
lamps, watches and clocks, radios and telephones,
tractors, and even a dentist's surgery.

Tennessee

Old Car Museum,
Dixie Gun Works, Inc.,
Highway 51 South,
Union City,
Tennessee
Open every day except Sunday 8.00–17.00
The 25 cars on show here, dating from 1909 to
1936, include a Waverley electric of the first-
named year, a 1914 Ford Model T raceabout, a
1927 Pierce Arrow, and 1930 and 1936 Packards.
Other exhibits on show are a collection of over
500 lamps, 50 hit-and-miss stationary gasoline
engines, and a fine display of popcorn
equipment – 15 popcorn popper steam engines,
three steam-operated popcorn poppers, and over
100 steam whistles.

* * *

Smoky Mountain Car Museum,
Highway 441,
Pigeon Forge,
Tennessee
Open every day May–October
Also evenings until 21.00 July–Labor Day
Brush, Cord L29, Cadillac, Duesenberg, Ford,
Hupmobile, Overland, Reo, and the rare
Marathon are represented among the 30 or so cars
in this collection.

SGV, 1912. Courtesy Boyertown Museum of Historic Vehicles, Boyertown, Pennsylvania

Texas

Pate Museum of Transportation,
Highway 377,
Cresson,
Texas
Open every day 9.00–17.00

The Pate Museum is devoted to all forms of historic wheeled transportation, from the Conestoga wagon of the pioneers to the aircraft and the motor car.

Vermont

* * *
Steamtown USA,
Bellows Falls,
Vermont
Open weekends only May 30–June 16
Open every day June 22–Labor Day
Open weekends only September 7–October 27
This railway museum, claimed to contain the largest collection of steam equipment in the United States, has over 100 locomotives and cars.

Virginia

Car and Carriage Caravan,
Luray Caverns,
Virginia
Open every day March 16–December 24
This is a museum of transportation providing a record of vehicles from the days of the oxcart through coaches to the motor car. There are about 77 motor vehicles, the cars including a Benz of the 1890s, a 1907 two-cylinder Buick and International Autowagon, the unique 1909 Middleby, a 1911 Hupmobile, 1912 Hudson, 1913 Stanley steamer, a Locomobile Gentleman's Speedster of 1914 (probably the most desirable of all), a 1924 Rolls Royce Silver Ghost that once belonged to Rudolph Valentino, and a front wheel drive Cord of 1930. In addition, a number of commercial and public service vehicles are on show, including fire engines. The museum has a remarkable collection of Fords, numbering 16 of models N, T, TT, and A.

Plymouth, 1950. Courtesy Joe Weatherly Stock Car Museum, Darlington, South Carolina

Wisconsin

Four Wheel Drive Museum and Historical
  Building,
FWD Corporation,
Clintonville,
Wisconsin
*Open weekdays May 1–November 1
10.00–12.00, 13.00–16.00*
This is a specialized museum, containing a
fascinating collection of American pioneers in the
field of four-wheel drive, among them the 1909
'Battleship', a 1932 Miller Special racing car, the
Butterworth FWD/ASB (also a racing car), and
examples of four-wheel drive trucks.

Brooks Stevens Automotive Museum
10325 N. Port Washington Road, 13-W,
Mequon,
Wisconsin
Open every day 10.00–17.00
The industrial designer, Brooks Stevens, who was
responsible for the 1952 Excalibur sports-racing
car and for a new version of it since then, as well
as for the Excalibur SS, an evocation of the
Mercedes-Benz of the 1920s, has created a
museum of about 50 cars near Milwaukee, beside
his Stevens Research and Development Center.
Some are on loan, and some belong to the
museum. They include a 1905 Cadillac (the oldest
on display), and, in complete contrast, the last
car made by Howard Marmon (1933). There are
Mercedes-Benz, Rolls Royce, and some racing
cars.

* * *

Sunflower Museum of Antique Cars,
Sunflower Lodge,
Lake Tomahawk,
Wisconsin
*Open every day May–October 1
10.00–12.00, 13.00–18.00*
Around 50 cars built between 1905 and 1932 are
on view in this museum; there is also an 1885
Manchester horsedrawn fire engine, and a 1915
Seagrave fire truck. The more unusual of the cars
include an International Harvester Buggy and
Autowagon, an early 12-cylinder Packard from
1916, a Detroit electric coupé of 1918, a very late
Stanley steamer (1921), a 1922 Columbia, a 1924
Case, a Viking V8 of 1930, and a 1934 eight-
cylinder Hupmobile.

* * *

Berman's Auto and Antique Museum,
Highway 14,
Oregon,
Wisconsin
Open April–October 7.00–21.00
There are over two dozen cars in this collection,
dating from 1902 onwards. Apart from a
Franklin and a 1916 Chevrolet, they include some
interesting variants on the humble Ford; a 1918
Model T with runners in place of the front wheels
and halftracks at the rear, for use in snow, a
miniature Model T for children, and a Model A
station wagon. Apart from the motor vehicles,
there are other fascinating relics of early
technology, such as a 1902 outboard motor,
typewriters of the same period, lawnmowers
from before 1900, vacuum cleaners of the 1870s,
and even dog-powered washing-machines.